CREW SIZE AND MARITIME SAFETY

Committee on the Effect of
Smaller Crews on Maritime Safety
Marine Board
Commission on Engineering and Technical Systems
National Research Council

NATIONAL ACADEMY PRESS
Washington, D.C.   1990

National Academy Press   •   2101 Constitution Avenue, N.W.   •   Washington, D.C. 20418

Library of Congress Cataloging-in-Publication Data

National Research Council (U.S.). Committee on the Effect of Smaller
    Crews on Maritime Safety.
        Crew size and maritime safety / Committee on the Effect of Smaller
    Crews on Maritime Safety, Marine Board, Commission on Engineering
    and Technical Systems, National Research Council.
            p.   cm.
        Includes bibliographical references.
        Includes index.
        ISBN 0-309-04375-1
        1. Ships—Manning. 2. Merchant marine—Safety measures.
    I. Title.
    VK221.N35   1990
    623.88'8—dc20

90-48577
CIP

Printed in the United States of America

DEDICATION

Rear Admiral William Michael Benkert, United States Coast Guard, retired, chaired the authoring committee until his death in December, 1989. Mike Benkert was a leading world spokesman for safety in maritime operations and protection of the marine environment. His friends and colleagues miss his wisdom, friendship, and indefatigable spirit. The work represented by this report could not have been completed without him and his outstanding leadership. The report is dedicated to his memory and to the furtherance of safety at sea everywhere.

Preface

Automation and mechanization of ships over the past three decades have resulted in continual reductions in the sizes of crews. Today the crew of a typical, recently built U.S.-flag vessel totals 20 to 24, compared with about 45 crew members 30 years ago. Some similarly designed foreign-flag vessels are manned by crews of 12 to 16. Highly automated foreign ships may operate with crews of 8 to 12.

Crew reductions accelerated in the 1980s as ship owners and operators throughout the world applied automation technology to make ships more efficient in the face of a serious shipping recession. The traditional shipping nations of Asia and northern Europe have been especially aggressive in substituting technology for personnel. Crew reductions by those national fleets came only after considerable study, review, and experimentation by the governments, operating companies, and labor organizations involved. The U.S. maritime industry has been slower to adopt these innovations.

While the crew reductions recently realized in the United States, and more dramatically in other nations, have improved operating efficiency, they have also raised concerns about their impacts on vessel and personnel safety.

ORIGIN OF THE STUDY

The U.S. Coast Guard, responsible for the safety of waterborne commerce, requested that the National Research Council (NRC) assess the safety implications of recent sharp reductions in crew sizes and advise on

vii

ways to evaluate and improve the safety of different manning levels. Accordingly, the NRC's Commission on Engineering and Technical Systems (CETS) convened the Committee on the Effect of Smaller Crews on Maritime Safety. Committee members were selected for their expertise and to achieve balanced experience and viewpoints. (Biographical information about committee members is presented in Appendix A.) The principle guiding the constitution of the committee and its work, consistent with NRC policy, was not to exclude the bias that might accompany expertise vital to the study, but to seek balance and fair treatment. The committee operated under the auspices of the Marine Board, a unit of CETS.

SCOPE OF THE STUDY

The committee's study encompassed all aspects of the safety issues raised by smaller crews. It was charged with:

• identifying the economic and technology changes that are causing manning reductions;

• forecasting the evolution of ship operating technology and the associated changes in crew organization and training;

• identifying the risks of smaller crews and assessing how they may be affected by changes in manning patterns;

• assessing the implications of smaller crews for training, skill levels, crewing patterns, and vessel operating technology; and

• developing a method for assessing the effects on safety of crew size, organization, and capabilities.

The study addressed mainly the manning and safety of U.S.-flag, ocean-going ships. Small passenger vessels, river tows, offshore supply boats, and fishing vessels were outside the study's scope.

STUDY METHODS

The committee sought experience and information from around the world. Ship operating companies, maritime labor organizations, national ship safety administrations, and international ship classification societies were contacted in person and through questionnaires to identify and document safety concerns, experience, and information sources. This effort included literature reviews; extended visits by the original chairman of the committee with senior managers from 10 major U.S. ship-operating companies to document and discuss their operating experience (Appendix D); an open meeting of the committee with leaders of 10 maritime labor organizations and discussions leading to documentation of maritime labor's perceptions concerning changes in shipboard crewing, management, and safety problems (Appendix C); visits by members of the committee and staff to three different ships with extensive automation and small crews and informal discussion with individual crew members; and interviews with more than 40 shipping executives, union officials, government shipping administrators, and human factors researchers in northern Europe conducted by a committee consultant.

The committee developed a computerized model for analyzing the manning of ships depending on their levels of automation, maintenance requirements, and crew skill levels. The model was validated with work records and other information from two vessels. The committee met five times over two years. The conclusions and recommendations represent the committee's consensus.

Acknowledgments

The committee benefited from the interest and contributions of a number of individuals and organizations. Admirals William Kime and Joel Sipes of the U.S. Coast Guard saw the need for a study of the safety implications of smaller crews and helped to set the course for the study. Norman Lemley of the U.S. Coast Guard provided effective liaison with the committee throughout its deliberations. Alex Landsburg represented the Maritime Administration in the committee's deliberations and was especially helpful in providing information on ship operating costs and human factors aspects. Sean Connaughton of the American Petroleum Institute and Joseph Cox of the American Institute of Merchant Shipping provided information and perspective.

Several experts gave time and energy to help the committee. Todd Grove, American Bureau of Shipping, addressed the committee on the "Ship of the Future." Raja Parasuraman, The Catholic University of America, spoke on "The State of the Art of Knowledge on Stress, Fatigue, and Boredom." Donald Sussman, Transportation Systems Center, shared current research concerning human factors aspects of ship operations. Alex Blanton of the law firm Dyer, Ellis, Joseph & Mills, provided a critical analysis of U.S. manning laws (Appendix F). Joseph Angelo of the U.S. Coast Guard shared his understanding of international developments. Tom Gillette and Richard Silloway, Exxon Shipping Co., and Daniel Steppe, American Institute of Merchant Shipping, assisted with the analysis of safety data.

Michael Gaffney, Cornell University, shared his rich knowledge of ship manning practices and conducted visits in northern Europe with ship manning experts. George Ireland, U.S. Coast Guard (retired), an expert in ship safety and regulation, made visits to ship operating companies and provided historical information on crew reductions in the U.S.-flag fleet. Lissa Martinez organized the roundtable with maritime labor representatives and helped coordinate other committee activities. Duncan Brown was an indefatigable rapporteur.

The committee is indebted to all who took the time to meet with committee members and otherwise respond to requests for information.

Contents

APPENDIXES

Executive Summary

Commercial vessels throughout the world have reduced the size of their crews dramatically in the past few decades. Modern, automated U.S.-flag ships have crews of about 20. Thirty years ago, vessels of comparable tonnage had twice that number. In contrast to American standards, the most technologically advanced ships in the world fleet today have crews of about 10.

The trend toward smaller crews has been accompanied by increasing concern for safety. While the impacts of crew reductions on operations have been carefully studied, the effect on safety has not received widespread attention. The most fundamental question is whether smaller crews degrade safety. A related issue is whether international and domestic statutes regulating crew size adequately protect workers, vessels, and the environment, and unduly restrict the adoption of new technology. Another issue is the Coast Guard's role in ensuring that foreign-flag vessels, with smaller crews than permitted under U.S. law, do not compromise safety in domestic waters.

WHAT ARE THE SAFETY CONCERNS?

Concerns about the effect of crew reductions on safety relate primarily to three operational considerations.

1. *Fatigue*: Will there be greater demands placed on crew members, and if so, will they be less alert? Or, will smaller crews work the same or fewer hours and thus be no more likely to suffer fatigue than larger crews?

2. *Training*: Will the crew be able to handle emergencies if automated systems fail? Will the crew be adequately trained to handle broader responsibilities and more sophisticated technology? Are higher or different levels of competence required?

3. *Maintenance*: Will crew reductions result in neglect of essential maintenance? To what extent will automation and technology advances improve reliability of ships' operating systems?

Lack of attention to these problems will raise the risk of injuries and vessel accidents with attendant social, economic and environmental costs.

WHAT IS THE SAFETY RECORD?

Available statistical information on maritime safety is inadequate to make definitive judgments about how various factors, including crew sizes, contribute to safety. Precise and uniformly defined information is needed to establish trends in safety performance and to make decisions about safety based on those trends. However, available safety statistics indicate the following:

• There has been a measurable and substantial reduction in vessel casualties (accidents) and personnel injuries during the past 20 years. These trends are consistent worldwide.

• During the same period, average crew size has declined substantially.

• Other factors have also changed. Technology has improved, operating procedures have been refined, and maritime operations have come under increased scrutiny by government and industry.

Vessel casualties and personnel injuries cannot be correlated with crew size based on available safety data. Thus it is not possible with available information to determine whether any causal relation—positive or negative—exists between crew size and safety. There are valid concerns about fatigue, training, and maintenance, but their effect on safety can be minimized through vigilance by management and labor organizations. Effective and thoroughly trained crew members and reliable automated ship systems become more important as crews are reduced.

ARE THERE HUMAN FACTORS CONCERNS?
HOW CAN THEY BE MANAGED?

The introduction of new technology in ships should consider not only technology, but human factors related to it. Ships should be viewed as sociotechnical systems, consisting of technologies, personnel, organizational structures, and an external environment. Change in any one of these subsystems may necessitate change in others. However, very few human factors studies have been conducted in the maritime field. Moreover, the Coast Guard does not have the necessary analytical tools to support decisions concerning the number of people needed to operate highly automated ships.

With appropriate training, organizational innovations, and ergonomic design, new vessel technology should not degrade safety. Training programs need to change as new technology is adopted, and licensing requirements need to be modernized. The general shift will be from specialized skills to a higher level of competence with a broader range of skills and more sophisticated technology.

HOW SHOULD SAFE CREW LEVELS BE ESTABLISHED?

In establishing safe crew levels, government and industry need to consider demands on crews on different vessels: specialized technologies, type of vessel service, the varied skills required, and the quality of management. Currently, the Coast Guard (and other national shipping safety administrations) relies in large part on laws, traditions, and informal guidance to determine manning levels. This piecemeal approach may have been effective when technology changed slowly and crews were larger, but today a consistent, internationally accepted method for determining safe manning is needed. The need for such a method will become more urgent with the worldwide adoption of new ship technology and innovative manning patterns. Systems engineering methods, including functional task analysis, offer an objective basis for determining crew sizes. The committee developed a systems engineering model to assess functions and tasks that could be used by the Coast Guard to determine safe manning levels for a variety of ship types and operating conditions.

A comprehensive international process for determining manning levels would include (1) a universally accepted statement of principles setting forth functional manning requirements, and (2) objective analysis tools to establish minimum safe manning scales. Such a process framework would help each vessel's flag state set manning levels and could be used by port states to assess whether vessels entering their waters are sufficiently manned. Internationally dictated manning scales are not desirable, since they would impose inappropriate standards on some ship operators and would hinder innovation for others.

DO U.S. MANNING LAWS NEED TO BE MODERNIZED?

U.S. manning laws have led to needless inefficiency and complexity and to unwarranted obstacles to the adoption of new ship operating technology.

Clearly, these statutes will effectively prohibit reducing crew sizes below current levels regardless of opportunities offered by technology. More importantly existing manning laws do not have a clearly identified emphasis on safety; in fact, they inhibit operational innovation without relation to safety aspects.

The Coast Guard has the authority to enforce safety requirements on foreign-flag vessels in U.S. ports. As a practical matter, the agency normally accepts manning levels established by other flag states as safe manning for entry into U.S. ports. However, manning decisions vary among the flag states. Consistent manning criteria among flag states and consistent enforcement authority by port states require a universally accepted analytical method for assessing safe manning similar to that developed by the committee. The International Maritime Organization (IMO) is the appropriate forum for developing such a method.

RECOMMENDATIONS

To foster safer shipping amid rapidly changing ship technologies, the committee recommends the following:

• Congress should modernize U.S. manning laws to allow innovation without degrading safety.

• The U.S. maritime industry, with the aid of the United States Department of Transportation, should implement a program to demonstrate the conditions under which reduced crew size can be considered safe. Among the demands on the crews that need to be evaluated are specialized technologies, type of vessel service, skills required, and the quality of management. Assessment and incorporation of worldwide developments to foster manning innovation should be an element of this program.

• The industry, with the aid of the U.S. Department of Transportation, should undertake a research program to determine how human factors such as fatigue and stress affect maritime safety.

• The Department of Transportation should gather, standardize, evaluate, and disseminate maritime safety data.

• The Coast Guard should use formal analytical methods, such as the approach developed by the committee, to make manning decisions. The goal should be to develop an internationally accepted method for establishing minimum safe manning levels.

The committee's complete conclusions and recommendations appear in Chapter 6.

CREW SIZE AND MARITIME SAFETY

1

Introduction

Thirty years ago, U.S.-flag commercial vessels typically went to sea with crews of more than 40 persons. Today, much larger U.S.-flag vessels depart on foreign voyages with crews of about 20. Many modern foreign vessels sail with crews in the middle to low teens. These reductions in manning levels reflect more than a century of gradual technical and organizational change. Sail gave way to steam, and steam has largely given way to diesel propulsion. Ship designers and builders have automated and mechanized many shipboard systems, adopted more durable coatings and paints, shifted some maintenance and cargo-handling duties to shore-based personnel, and made other transitions toward more efficient manning.

In the United States, these innovations have involved the Coast Guard directly in setting manning levels in the past two decades. In the past each vessel's Coast Guard-issued Certificate of Inspection (COI) specified the minimum deck, engine, and radio complements necessary for safe navigation. In practice, ships typically carried up to twice the minimum required crew members, through collective bargaining between companies and their unions. With the advent of diesel propulsion, automation, and other labor-saving measures in the late 1960s, labor-management contracts began to settle on the COI requirements as minimum manning scales. Thus, Coast Guard manning decisions are taking on ever greater significance.

These changes are far from having run their course. Ship technology is developing at an accelerating pace throughout the world. The accompanying organizational innovations in the past few years have gone beyond straightforward crew reductions in some nations to reorganizations of crews and reallocation of tasks. The traditional division of crews into deck and engine departments, for example, is fading, as owners and operators seek to make the most efficient use of labor and new technology.

In general, improved operating economics is the objective. Technological improvements, including automation, have resulted in improved fuel efficiency, higher reliability, and lower labor costs. In pursuing cost competitiveness, however, the U.S. merchant marine has been faced with foreign competition that has been even more intent on reducing crews. European and Asian operators have led the way for several decades. Europeans undertook the first major postwar crew reductions in response to labor shortages during the worldwide shipping expansion of the 1960s and early 1970s. More reductions came in the 1980s, as a globally depressed shipping market drove operators in many countries—often with the aid of government research and development programs—to cut costs and streamline operations by further automating ships. In the 1970s and 1980s, operators in Japan, Taiwan, and other Asian nations became leaders in applying ship technology and reducing crews.

In that sense, this report does not address a new concept. Many technological and organizational innovations now being examined in the United States have been tested thoroughly by other nations' fleets. Comparable progress in the United States, however, has been inhibited by a traditional lack of coordinated and shared effort on the parts of government, industry, and labor. It is not possible to approach optimization of manning without a realistic collaboration involving these three sectors. Nonetheless, the progress that has been made in the United States clearly demonstrates, albeit on a limited basis, what can be achieved.

One emerging problem is the legal and regulatory framework of U.S. shipping. Unlike other statutes, those applying to the manning of ships lack a broad statement of regulatory purpose or policy that can be interpreted by regulators as technology advances and socioeconomic goals change. Instead, they specify manning practices based on outmoded shipboard divisions of labor (such as the increasingly obsolescent distinction between deck and engine departments) and watch-keeping practices (such as the requirement to employ enough personnel to keep three watches in traditional watch-keeping positions, even though most engine department personnel no longer stand watches). These requirements limit the efficiency with which shipboard labor can be used, without providing the safety assurance that is the purpose of regulation.

Many nations have revised their manning statutes and regulations to accommodate these moves toward operating efficiency. Others, including the United States, have not. The result is that identical modern vessels may carry widely varying crew sizes depending on the flag they fly. Since the Coast Guard is responsible for ensuring that foreign-flag vessels do not present undue risks to U.S. ports and waterways, the agency is put in the anomalous position of permitting foreign vessels to enter U.S. ports with crews that would be illegal under U.S. safety regulations.

To protect the environment and the safety of ships and seafarers, the Coast Guard should be authorized by law to update its regulatory practices. A regulatory framework that enforces half-century-old practices on a rapidly evolving industry can support neither safety nor competitiveness. Nor does it provide a rational basis for U.S. participation in international debate on manning practices.

SAFETY CONCERNS

Some operators, maritime labor unions, and regulators have voiced concerns that reductions in crews, if not managed properly, could degrade safety. Some believe maintenance is widely neglected. Others say fatigue—a perennial concern aboard ship—has grown more widespread and more serious. Still others worry that the elimination of entry-level positions has degraded the skills of unlicensed crew members.

These concerns, if substantiated, would be expected to manifest themselves in increased accident rates, yet data to prove or disprove them are scarce. Available casualty and accident data bases are insufficient for firm judgments, and no full-scale statistical study of the problem has been done. As will be shown in Chapter 2, while rates of ship casualties and personnel injuries have declined steadily during the crew reductions of the past 20 years, the contribution of manning practices to this safety improvement is obscured by the fact that many new technological advances and safety requirements, with no bearing on manning, have occurred simultaneously. Anecdotal evidence of growing safety problems is compelling to many, but there is a lack of substantiating data to support or refute these perceptions.

The methodical, step-by-step crew reductions of other nations' fleets, backed by years of experiment and analysis, lend confidence to the view that properly managed crew reductions need not compromise safety. Transferring that technology and operating practice to the U.S. maritime environment, however, will require comprehensive attention not only to the technology and personnel practices of the U.S.-flag fleet, but also to its regulatory and legal framework.

MANNING REDUCTIONS IN THE WORLD'S FLEETS, 1950s-1980s

Since World War II, several generations of vessels have been launched. Advances in automation, mechanization, and reallocation of crew members' responsibilities, have each permitted reductions in crew levels.

All of these developments have been pioneered by Western European and Japanese operators, often with government assistance. The late 1950s saw containerization of cargo, and the late 1960s saw the first engine room automation; some engine room personnel were rendered redundant, while most of the rest were relieved of watch-standing responsibilities. The mid-1980s produced highly automated vessels like the products of the German "Ship of the Future" program: with propulsion, navigation, and communication controls centralized on the bridge; engine room layouts arranged for easy maintenance; and installation of a variety of automated safety equipment. These vessels were designed for crews as small as 11. (Those operating under the American flag, however, carry crews of 21.)

In the late 1980s, European and Japanese governments supported even greater automation, centralizing navigation, engine control, communications, and administrative functions on the bridge (which came to be called a "ship operation center"), and more mechanization and automation throughout the vessel. Corresponding changes in crew members' job assignments were made in efforts to make the most effective use of both ship technology and labor.

Table 1-1 compares the manning patterns of four representative generations of ships, from the U.S.-flag steamship of the 1960s to the highly sophisticated Japanese "Pioneer" series. To illustrate the effect of current U.S. manning statutes and labor contracts, two manning scales are shown for the German "Ship of the Future," one for German-flag operation and the other for U.S.-flag operation.

The First Generation

Until the late 1960s, most ocean-going U.S.-flag cargo vessels were powered by steam and had separate engine and boiler rooms. The engine department on such a ship was typically manned by a chief engineer, a first assistant engineer, a second assistant engineer, three third assistant engineers, two electricians, three fire/watertenders, three oilers, and three wipers each standing three watches. Three licensed engineers, the fire/watertenders, and the oilers stood watches, four hours on and eight off, round the clock.

The steward's department had seven to nine members. Food was purchased in bulk quantities—sides of beef, bags of flour, and boxes of fruit and vegetables—and reduced to meals by a staff of cooks, bakers, and utility messmen. Meals were served restaurant style. A room steward cleaned officers' quarters.

The deck department consisted of as many as 18 members: a master, a chief mate, a second mate, three third mates, a boatswain, six able-bodied seamen (ABs), three ordinary seamen (OSs), two day men, and a carpenter. A mate, two ABs, and one OS stood each watch. The ABs and OSs also

TABLE 1-1 Crew Reductions, 1960s-1980s

	U.S.-flag Steamship, 1960s	U.S.-flag, Maintenance Department, Late 1980s	German "Ship of the Future" Early 1980s F.R.G.*	U.S.	Japanese "Pioneer" Ship Late 1980s
Master	1	1	1	1	1
Chief Mate	1	1	1	1	
2nd Mate	1	1	1	1	
3rd Mates	3	1		1	
Unlicensed deck personnel	13	3		6	
Chief Engineer	1	1	1	1	1
1st Asst. Eng.	1	1	1	1	
2nd Asst. Eng.	1	2		1	
3rd Asst. Eng.	3			1	
Electrician	1		1		
Boatswain	1		1		
Unlicensed eng. personnel	9			3	
Maintenance personnel		5			
Gen. purpose crew			4		4
Dual-licensed officer					4
Steward's/catering personnel	8	4	2	3	1
Radio officer	1	1	1	1	
TOTAL	45	21	14	21	11

*German manning scale from Grove (1989), p. 4.

did deck maintenance and anchored, moored, and unmoored the ship. A radio officer completed the crew.

Progress Toward the Unattended Engine Room

The initial postwar reductions in crew size were brought about by making vessel machinery self-regulating, centralizing controls, and automating certain functions. These developments culminated in the so-called "unattended engine room," which can be monitored from the bridge or other remote locations, and requires no watch-standing crew members in the engine room itself.

Automated Boiler Controls

The first engine department crew reduction in the postwar United States, in 1964, was enabled by installing automatic controls on propulsion boilers. Boilers so equipped could be operated without constant human attendance, and thus allowed the requirement for three fireman/watertenders (one for each watch) to be removed from the vessel's Certificate of Inspection (COI). A vessel with automated boiler controls still required constant attendance by an engineer and an oiler for each watch.

In the early 1970s, the oilers were relieved of watch-standing by centralization of machinery controls and installation of propulsion controls in the pilothouse. A single licensed engineer thus stood each watch alone. On oil tankers, the same technology—fluidic systems, electronic solid-state controls, and data logging devices—was also used for cargo pump controls.

The Unattended Engine Room

Diesel propulsion came into common use in the late 1960s to early 1970s with utilization of slow-speed diesel plants. Greater economy than steam propulsion and better adaptability to full automation were the driving forces for this trend. Slow-speed diesel propulsion entered U.S.-flag fleets in the 1970s. It let operators design machinery spaces for "periodically unattended" operation, with computers to monitor and control vital systems. Periodically unattended machinery spaces could be unmanned for prolonged periods of time, and therefore did not require round-the-clock attendance by a licensed engineer.

This innovation was accompanied by further crew reductions (for example, the elimination of one or more third assistant engineers). Its most important effect, however, was to free crew members from watch-standing, allowing them to do other jobs, such as maintenance; in this way it led eventually to the creation (in the United States) of the maintenance department, a more recent innovation discussed later in this chapter. In Japan, the Federal Republic of Germany, Norway, the Netherlands, and other countries, it opened the way for more sweeping change.

Innovations in the Deck Department

By a variety of labor-saving measures, vessel operators in the 1970s did away with the need for daymen, carpenters, and most ordinary seamen.

Elimination of the Relief Person on Navigation Watches

In the deck department, labor-saving devices and the increasing use of shore-based personnel for maintenance led to further crew reductions. For example, navigation watch-standing on the bridge traditionally required a licensed officer as well as a lookout and a helmsman (generally both ABs). A third unlicensed person (generally an OS) was used for relief helmsman and to serve as an additional lookout when needed. By the early 1970s, the relief person had been eliminated on many ships by placing sanitary facilities and drinking water on the same deck as the pilothouse, installing watch-call systems (which wake the members of the next scheduled watch), and other measures.

Mechanization of the Deck

Mooring, unmooring, and anchoring also became less labor intensive with the installation of constant-tension winches with strategically located controls, as well as lightweight synthetic mooring lines. New paints and coatings diminished the need for chipping and painting. Automated hatch covers also eliminated the need for much hand work.

Containerization of Cargo

The containerization of cargo in the 1960s and 1970s further reduced crew tasks and eliminated most cargo handling by crew members. For example, containerization reduced the need for deck maintenance by eliminating most shipboard cargo-handling equipment.

Technology in the Steward's Department

The steward's department was also reduced by the application of technology. Microwave ovens and prepackaged meals eliminated most food preparation and service. Officers began to make their own beds and clean their own rooms. Microcomputers came into use for inventory control. Steward's departments aboard U.S.-flag vessels now are typically staffed by three or four persons, and often fewer.

The Maintenance Department Aboard U.S.-Flag Vessels: Response to a Regulatory Impasse

In many foreign countries, advancing technology and accompanying reductions in manning have prompted shipping companies, with the support of safety regulators and unions, to break down some of the traditional departmental boundaries and eliminate the division of crews into watches. Many European and Asian ships, for example, have "general purpose" unlicensed crew members, who may work at either engine or deck responsibilities as needed. Some also use dual-qualified "watch officers," who have both engine and deck training (Grove, 1989).

In the United States, the flexibility necessary to make effective and safe use of personnel and new technology is not available under the manning statutes administered by the U.S. Coast Guard (46 U.S.C. § 8103-9308). Those statutes, developed over many years on the basis of traditional practice, require the strict division of personnel aboard ship into deck and engine departments, even though it would be more efficient to assign them more flexibly (46 U.S.C. § 8104(e)(1)). In addition, they require division of those who serve in the deck and engine departments into three watches, although increasing numbers of shipboard workers do not stand watches (46 U.S.C. § 8104). To provide some flexibility, the Coast Guard in the 1970s acquiesced to the establishment by the industry of the position of deck/engine mechanic. These day workers were assigned to the engine department but could be used both on deck and in machinery spaces. They usually had unlicensed engine training, as qualified members of the engine department (QMEDs).

The Coast Guard in the late 1980s began to certificate some vessels with shipboard "maintenance departments." Maintenance departments are intended to provide the flexibility of assignments necessary to achieve manning levels of 20 or less, within the bounds of existing law. Maintenance personnel are permitted by the Coast Guard to perform both engine and deck jobs, as well as routine maintenance. They are not divided into watches.

Maintenance departments generally have five members. Coast Guard policy requires generally that two members be QMEDs and the other three ABs. (Two of the AB positions may be filled by specially trained OSs.) Some vessels have been authorized to operate with three, rather than five, maintenance persons, dispensing with the two QMEDs. The department may be directed at different times by the master, the chief mate, and the chief engineer, but the master retains ultimate authority in allocating crew members' efforts.

The result of the Coast Guard's authorization of maintenance departments was to facilitate the distribution of labor more evenly between deck and engine personnel. Automation of engine rooms had done away with watch-standing in the engine department, thereby eliminating the need for some unlicensed engine department personnel. Meanwhile, complements of deck personnel, responsible for labor intensive but sporadic tasks such as mooring, remained relatively numerous. The establishment of maintenance departments permitted this unequal balance of labor to be corrected (personal communication, Sean Connaughton, February 6, 1990).

State of the Art and the Decade Ahead

In the 1980s, again, operators overseas have led U.S.-flag fleets in manning-related innovations. This phase of innovation has emphasized the centralized control of all ship functions on the bridge, with more comprehensive automation of navigation, engine control, cargo operations, safety and emergency systems, and communications. These changes have been accompanied by reallocations of crew members' responsibilities and dramatic crew reductions and have been supported by careful analysis and experimentation (Grove, 1989; Yamanaka and Gaffney, 1988).

In state-of-the-art ships the bridge has become a "ship operation center," housing controls and monitors for all essential vessel functions. Many routine navigational tasks, such as chart updating, position plotting, and steering, have been automated: For example, aboard the German "Ship of the Future," eight of which were built by early 1989, the ship's position is determined automatically by a computer that integrates information from satellite navigation systems and other equipment. The position is displayed as a dot of light on an electronic chart. Ballast is adjusted from the bridge while the ship is underway. Logs, reports, certificates, documents, and letters are computerized, with electronic mail links via satellite to shore (Grove, 1989; Kristiansen et al., 1989).

The levels of automation in these ships, and other advanced vessels, not only reduce the need for the helmsman and—in good visibility—the lookout on the bridge, but also reduce the need for deck and engine personnel generally. The result is that some foreign vessels operate with very small crews. Some large Norwegian vessels sail with crews of 8 to 12 (Kristiansen et al., 1989). The Japanese "Pioneer" vessels have 11-person crews (Grove, 1989; Yamanaka and Gaffney, 1988). The German "Norasia" vessels carry 16 persons, but are designed to operate with 12 (Gaffney, 1989, p.8). Japan, which has carried out the world's most ambitious reduced manning program, has mounted a research program to design a fully automated vessel, capable of operation from sea buoy to sea buoy by a single person or, ultimately, an advanced computer (Hamada, 1989).

These radical manning reductions have led some European and Asian shipping companies to eliminate or blur departmental distinctions with "general purpose" unlicensed ratings and dual-qualified officers (trained in both engine and deck skills). Further reductions may blur some distinctions between licensed and unlicensed personnel; in Japan, for example, some specially trained senior ratings already are permitted to serve in charge of bridge and engine watches (Yamanaka and Gaffney, 1988). In the Netherlands, some ratings supervise anchor watches.

West Germany

General-purpose Ratings. Since 1987, the West German shipping industry has provided only general-purpose training for its unlicensed personnel, eliminating separate deck and engine specialties. These personnel are known as ship's mechanics and can advance to the position of ship's foreman.

In preparation for this change, Hapag-Lloyd AG, a German shipping

company, experimented over 18 months with 4 ships manned by 18 crew
members, of whom 7 were general-purpose ratings. The success of this
experiment led the German government in 1984 to change its manning
regulations, allowing the crew of even the largest ship to be reduced to 19
persons, provided that manning was based on the general-purpose concept.

Dual-qualified Officers. To meet the operating requirements of state-
of-the-art ships with controls and monitors centralized on the bridge, the
German shipping industry has recently developed the concept of the "ship
management officer." This officer would be responsible for the entire
ship—cargo, navigation, and maintenance—and would need both technical
knowledge and expertise in seamanship. A ship manned by such officers
would have a master and four ship management officers; at present, German
ships carry three deck and two engineer officers, in addition to the master
(Froese, 1989). In 1986 as a first step in that direction, the industry—with
government support—began offering officers with existing top-level deck
or engine licenses the opportunity to earn medium-level credentials in the
opposite specialties.

Japan

Japanese shipping companies, perhaps, have gone further toward departmental integration than those of any other flag. The initial experiments,
in 1979, were succeeded by a carefully planned sequence of steps toward a
new "Hypothetical Image of Seafarers." The goal was the complete elimination of departmental distinctions, and the substitution of a shipboard
management team.

In 1981, the first phase of these experiments began aboard several
new vessels whose bridges were fitted with monitoring and control systems
for propulsion machinery and safety systems; remote controls for mooring
winches, cargo-handling equipment, and ballast; and satellite position location and communication systems. The distinction between deck and engine
departments was removed for unlicensed personnel, and junior officers' positions (third officer and third engineer) were filled by dual-qualified watch
officers. This pattern of organization, with an 18-person standard crew, was
incorporated in the manning laws in 1983, and its application was widened
to more diverse types of ships. By April 1985, 145 ships were operating
with 18-person crews (Anonymous, 1989).

Meanwhile, an experiment with 16-person crews had begun in 1982
aboard vessels with additional automated cargo-handling and navigation
equipment. Watch officers replaced engine and deck officers up to the level
of second officer and second engineer. In addition, specially trained ratings
were used as watch-keepers on the bridge. The success of this experiment

resulted in this manning pattern being put into law in 1986 and applied to 98 ships (Anonymous, 1989).

Also in 1986, experiments with 14-person crews were begun. The vessels' bridges were further automated, with all functions of the deck, engine, and radio watches centralized in a ship operation center configuration, and with additional labor-saving devices for mooring and unmooring.

The 11-person Pioneer Ship experiments began in April 1987 aboard 7 new vessels. The main technical innovations were the placement of auxiliary engine and navigation controls on the wing of the bridge, a labor-saving galley, and "labor-saving oil processing devices with sufficient disposal facility" (Anonymous, 1989).

The Netherlands

Dutch shipping companies pioneered the use of general-purpose ratings and dual-qualified officers, beginning as much as 20 years ago. Dutch officers are trained and licensed with major and minor specialties (navigation and technical) and are expected soon to be completely integrated as "maritime officers" or "ship managers" (Cross, 1988).

Highly trained ship mechanics with general-purpose qualifications have been employed aboard Dutch ships since the late 1970s. However, they reportedly are generally used in traditional engine and deck specialties, since there has been too little highly skilled work available on today's modern automated ships. Vessels may carry one or two ship mechanics to maintain mechanical systems. More recently, they have been assigned as core crew aboard vessels manned largely with unskilled Third World crew members. In the guise of ship technicians, they may assume supervisory responsibilities in such cases.

Two Models for Manning Innovation

In developing new concepts of vessel manning, operators have generally adopted one of two general approaches to the allocation of management responsibilities between ship and shore. The first might be called the "airline model," which involves shifting management and maintenance responsibilities from ship to shore, with the crew responsible mainly for operating the vessel from port to port. The other approach is to transfer management responsibilities from shore to ship to raise efficiency and improve the quality of officers' jobs. A management team typically is formed consisting of the master and department heads and sometimes junior officers and senior ratings. The team may be responsible for operating expenses and budget, personnel, and maintenance, within overall guidelines set by company headquarters. The data and voice capabilities of modern communications systems permit adequate exchange of information between ship and shore.

In this scheme, the chief engineer becomes a particularly important part of the team, responsible for planning and scheduling maintenance of all mechanical systems.

MAKING THE BEST USE OF TECHNOLOGY

Vessels now entering some U.S.-flag fleets embody the highest technology available worldwide. For example, the European-built C-10 container ships recently put into service by American President Lines—comprehensively automated ships of the future with all control systems centralized on the bridge—are designed to operate with 11-member crews. Under current laws, regulatory policies, and labor-management contracts, however, they sail with crews of 21. The challenge to operators and regulators is to use available technology effectively, without compromising safety. At present there are three major obstacles to this goal.

1. The legal basis of manning decisions is antiquated and needs to be reexamined; its rigidity in the face of technological change (notably the division of crew into three watches and the prohibition of crossing departmental lines) has become glaringly obvious.

2. The Coast Guard has no human factors models to guide its manning judgments in vessel certification or accident investigation. With further crew reductions, the agency will need far better information and analytical tools to make manning decisions. In general, systems engineering and human factors methods are used little in the shipping industry. Research in all these areas is needed, with special attention to the unique features of work aboard ships, such as stress and fatigue.

3. The available data on vessel safety as a function of manning are inadequate to judge the safety of current crew levels, let alone those envisioned for the future. Further data and statistical studies will be required to confirm or eliminate those concerns.

The Need for a Systems Approach to Manning Assessments

In the United States, thus far, crew reductions have been accomplished by straightforward substitutions of technology for human beings, with little change in traditional work functions or overall work organization beyond the consolidation of responsibilities described above. However, the pace of change is continuing. Shipping companies have moved aggressively toward greater efficiency by automating and mechanizing their vessels. Resulting crew levels are approaching the minimum levels within the current U.S. manning statutes. Further crew reductions will depend on more radical changes in crew organization, such as general-purpose unlicensed personnel permitted to work in both engine and deck departments and dual-qualified officers who combine engine and deck training.

In the interest of efficiency and safety, therefore, it would be useful to make a fresh and more comprehensive analysis of ship operations. With careful attention to workers' functions and the fundamental ship design, vessels could be developed to run safely with much smaller crews. Such studies have been carried out in countries around the world and the results are already seeing service (Grove, 1989; Yamanaka and Gaffney, 1988). Chapter 4 outlines a technique for making a thorough functional analysis of the tasks that need to be done aboard ship and the potential for automation.

SUMMARY

The rapid pace of innovation in the shipping industry is continuing worldwide. New technology has permitted many U.S.-flag ship operators to reduce crews by nearly half since the 1950s. In the future, however, innovation will be hampered by an antiquated statutory framework governing manning decisions.

The safety effects of U.S. crew reductions are imperfectly understood. Although it is clear that casualty and personnel accident rates have declined during the same period that crews have been reduced, no definitive study of the effects of these smaller crews has been made. The information on which to base such a study is not readily available.

The history of manning innovation in Western Europe and Asia offers grounds for confidence. Each phase of the crew reductions in Japan, West Germany, the Netherlands, and elsewhere has been preceded by study and experimentation to ensure that safety has not been degraded. Crew reductions in the United States should build on this experience, with appropriate attention to the unique features of the U.S.-flag fleet.

Although the most fundamental question continues to be whether the move toward smaller crews in U.S.-flag fleets has tended to degrade safety, an important directly related issue is whether the current statutory framework adequately protects workers, vessels, and the environment, and whether it unduly restricts the adoption of new technology.

Also at issue is the Coast Guard's role in ensuring that foreign-flag vessels, with smaller crews than those permitted by U.S. regulations, do not compromise safety in U.S. waters. The Coast Guard's dilemma is that in the absence of clear violations of manning levels as dictated by flag states, the Coast Guard must accept the decisions of foreign flag states concerning manning of their vessels.

REFERENCES

American President Lines. 1989. Labor contract. Report to the National Research Council Committee on the Effect of Smaller Crews on Maritime Safety. Marine Board, National Research Council, Washington, D.C. December 21.

Anonymous. 1989. The modernization of the seafarer's system in Japan. Paper presented at Maritime Training Forum Europe '89, Amsterdam, June 20.

Connaughton, S. 1987. Coast Guard merchant vessel manning. Paper presented at 1987 Ship Operations, Management and Economics International Symposium, U.S. Merchant Marine Academy, September 17-18.

Cross, S. J. 1988. Nautical training in the Netherlands: Present and future. *Seaways*

Froese, Jens. 1989. Training for advanced ships. Paper presented at Maritime Training Forum Europe '89, Amsterdam, June 20. Meeting sponsored by Nautical Institute and Marine Research Institute Netherlands.

Gaffney, Michael E. 1989. Effective manning at American President Lines. Report from American President Lines to U.S. Department of Transportation, Maritime Administration, Office of Technology Assessment. Cooperative Agreement No. MA-11727, Report No. MA-RD-840-89008. June 6.

Grove, T. W. 1989. U.S.-flag ship of the future: Concepts, features and issues. Paper presented at 1989 Spring Meeting and STAR Symposium, Society of Naval Architects and Marine Engineers, New Orleans, April.

Hamada, Noboru. 1989. A few proposals on the ship technology for the 21st century. Conference record, 15th Meeting of the U.S.-Japan Marine Facilities Panel. U.S./Japan Cooperative Program in Natural Resources. May.

Kristiansen, Svein, Egil Rensvik, and Lars Mathisen. 1989. Integrated total control of the bridge. Proceedings of the Society of Naval Architects and Marine Engineers Annual Meeting, New York, November 15-18.

National Research Council. 1984. Effective manning of the U.S. merchant fleet. Washington, D.C.: National Academy Press.

Schuffel, H., J. P. A. Boer, and L. van Breda. 1989. The ship's wheelhouse of the nineties: The navigation performance and mental workload of the officer of the watch. Journal of the Institute of Navigation 42:1(60-72). Jan.

Yamanaka, Keiko, and Michael Gaffney. 1988. Effective manning in the Orient. Report from American President Lines to U.S. Department of Transportation, Maritime Administration, Office of Technology Assessment. Cooperative Agreement No. MA-11727, Report No. MA-RD-770-87052. March 15.

2

Safety Experience with Smaller Crews

Recent reductions in crew sizes aboard Asian and northern European vessels have been preceded by extensive government sponsored programs to define, through careful step-by-step experimentation, the potential operational impacts. In the United States, less significant reductions in crew sizes and discussions of further reductions have been met with legitimate concern about their impact on maritime safety. However, the United States has not seen a comparable effort by government, industry, and labor to address this concern through comprehensive analysis and experimentation.

Safety concerns expressed over crew reductions relate primarily to three operational considerations.

1. *Fatigue*: Will there be greater demands placed on the remaining crew members, and if so will there be a reduction in alertness negatively impacting safety of the ship or its crew? Or, will the overall impact of changes hold even or reduce working hours and/or fatigue levels for the remaining crew?

2. *Training*: With the higher degree of automation (often used to justify crew reductions), will the remaining crew be able to handle emergencies if automated systems fail? Are higher or different levels of competence required? Will the crew be adequately trained for the new conditions?

3. *Maintenance*: Will crew reductions result in the neglect of essential maintenance? To what extent will better equipment, more durable coatings, riding maintenance crews, and other measures compensate by improving the reliability of equipment?

Lack of attention to these problems will raise the risk of injuries and vessel accidents with attendant social, economic, and environmental costs.

The U.S. Coast Guard, as the regulatory body charged with protecting the public interest in such matters, has addressed these questions each time it has been asked to set or revise the minimum manning levels specified by a vessel's Certificate of Inspection (COI). To make these judgments requires an objective and stable regulatory framework based on adequate safety statistics and a clear understanding of the automation technologies now being installed.

The Coast Guard must also take into account variations from ship to ship and from operator to operator. The nation's and the world's fleets are highly varied. Manning practices that are acceptable aboard a well-managed, well-maintained ship with a well-trained crew and appropriate automation and safety equipment may be unacceptable aboard a vessel without these advantages.

These regulatory judgments are especially challenging where the Coast Guard must carry out its responsibility to prevent unsafe practices by foreign-flag vessels in U.S. ports. Some flags have much higher casualty rates than others (Ponce, 1990). (The United States, despite its aging fleet, has one of the better safety records in this regard.) Although the Coast Guard has legal authority to inspect foreign-flag vessels for any and all safety deficiencies, the agency in practice does not object to manning practices that conform to vessels' flag state requirements (see Chapter 5).

Accidents are discrete events that are often highly visible and readily recounted as evidence of declining safety. Public concerns raised by them are often valid and may be difficult to respond to. Less evident and certainly less prone to publicity are the data relating to safety performance over an extended period of time and across a broad spectrum of operations. Over the past 20 years, the industry has experienced a general improvement in its casualty and personnel injury rates. While not perfect in either comprehensiveness or standardization of reporting format, such data are currently the best indicator of whether safety regulations and systems to promote or improve safety are achieving their intended objectives.

Unfortunately, however, the available data bases on casualties, accidents, and oil spills do not readily yield information on crew sizes of the vessels involved. A clear understanding of the safety record of smaller crews will require first a substantial data collection effort—an effort that was beyond this committee's means. In the future, the proprietors of the data bases should take steps to ensure that they capture crew size information.

THE PROBLEM OF QUANTIFYING MARITIME SAFETY

The problem of assessing maritime safety goes beyond the lack of crew size data. Determining the overall safety impacts of moves toward smaller crews requires estimating not only the associated marginal increase or decrease in the frequency of casualties, accidents, and environmental pollution incidents, but also the impacts of those events on people, property, and the environment. The information on which to base such an assessment is subject to great uncertainty. It is at present inadequate for development of sound conclusions.

The most fundamental problem is that the impacts of casualties, personnel accidents, and environmental pollution incidents are highly varied, and thus difficult to assess and compare. Property damage, environmental damage, and human pain or death are very different things. Assessing and comparing impacts of maritime safety lapses must therefore be largely subjective. In practice, regulatory priorities of this kind are established by policy decisions, reflecting the values society places on the various potential losses involved.

The frequency of such incidents, in contrast, are quantifiable, given adequate information. Several organizations maintain records of these events both domestically and worldwide. For example, data on the numbers of casualties, personnel injuries, and oil spills per year are easily obtained. However, this information by itself is inadequate for meaningful statistical estimates of the contributions of vessel manning to the safety record. First, the available data bases do not include information on vessels' manning in computer-searchable form.

In addition, they do not generally offer information on the many other variables and causal factors that interact to determine the safety record of an individual vessel. Management practices (e.g., maintenance, training, and scheduling), extent of compliance with regulatory requirements, the performance of those entrusted with operating and navigating vessels, and the service to which the vessel is put (its trade and routes); all must be known or statistically estimated before the causal role of manning in safety performance can be assessed.

Finally, there is no general agreement on an appropriate measure of exposure to hazards. Casualty and accident data must be related to an exposure variable. One obvious approach might be to compare the percentage of a given flag's (or a given fleet's) tankers experiencing accidents to the corresponding percentage of the worldwide fleet experiencing the same class of accidents. However, this comparison may be misleading, since tankers of different flags may have markedly different services and routes, thereby encountering different hazards. Studies thus far have used at least three approximations of exposure to hazards: port calls, tons delivered, and ton-miles. These measures yield very different estimates of accident frequencies and can yield different rankings of risk. For example, as tanker size increases the rate of accidents and pollution incidents increases when tabulated by port call, but decreases when tabulated by ton of cargo delivered (Meade et al., 1981). Furthermore, collection and analysis of exposure data is not routine; obtaining and working with it can be time consuming. Development of maritime exposure data bases is required.

Accurate maritime safety assessments require precise, reliable, and highly detailed data on vessels, casualties, accidents, and pollution incidents. In addition, identifying trends requires intimate knowledge of the validity and variability of data from different sources and complex multivariate analysis. At present, such a treatment cannot be supported by the available data and analytic methods.

Lack of Reliable Data

The committee attempted to assess the possible effects of smaller crews on ship safety by analyzing data gathered and maintained by the U.S. Coast Guard, Lloyd's Register of Shipping, shipping companies, and industry organizations. It compiled records of reported ship casualties and personnel injuries from these sources and tried to relate these to information on crew size. Unfortunately, it became apparent that no adequate body of such data is available in the public domain. Neither government nor industry has collected and maintained accident and casualty data that can be readily paired with that on crew size, training, or organization. Developing such data in the future will require a worldwide initiative to record crew information with every report of a casualty or accident and to store the information in such a way that researchers can analyze it.

The most important obstacle to this attempt was the fact that none of the maritime casualty data bases has crew size coded to allow tabulation of records on this basis. For example, although the Coast Guard's form for "Report of Marine Accident, Report of Death (CG-2692)" provides for the entry of the number of persons on board, this information is not recorded in the ship casualty (CASMAIN) and pollution incident (PIRS) data bases that the Coast Guard uses to access accident data. (In fact, a manual review of the raw accident reports revealed that more than one-fourth of the reports provided no indication of crew numbers.)

Lloyd's Register of Shipping does not collect crew size data in any of its ship or casualty records. The Marine Index Bureau comes closest to providing the desired information. Owing to its billing policy, this private agency has crew size data for each member company's ships. This administrative feature theoretically would allow the agency to correlate member companies' reported shipboard accident data with crew size. However, the requirement of strict anonymity of the reporting companies and crews precludes follow-up analysis of such data.

An adequate analysis of maritime safety, in the committee's view, requires the direct comparison of safety data for similar ships being manned at low and higher levels. Such comparisons within an operator's own fleet, or on the same ships at different times and different levels of manning, seem most appropriate, since they avoid attributing to manning safety differences that may be due to other factors, such as management, maintenance support, or operating conditions. Minimally, comparisons should be sought that ensure that high- and low-manned ships from different fleets are matched by size, age, trade, nationality, shore support, and operating costs.

An excellent, albeit limited, example of the kind of comparison to be desired is the case, discussed more fully below, of a 16-vessel containership fleet whose operator collected consistent personnel injury data over six years during which crews were reduced from 34 to 21. During this period, the annual rate of injuries per crew member remained stable. While this isolated case demonstrates the possibility of making meaningful statistical assessments, it is grossly insufficient as a basis for general conclusions. Comparable data covering a broader range of casualties and accidents and a larger cross-section of the world's fleets are needed.

Because the vast majority of marine casualty data are incomplete and unsystematic compared with the previous example, the committee conducted limited trial investigations of existing data to determine whether the influence of crew size could be studied in a practical manner. In one trial, a small sample of vessels known to be operated with crews of 20 or fewer was extracted by name from the U.S. Coast Guard's data bases (including the Coast Guard's copy of the Lloyd's Register files). Information was obtained on reported spills and hull or machinery failures for 20 U.S. tankers and integrated tug-barges (ITBs) between 1975 and 1987.

Although the average incidences of spills and failures per ship were obtainable, there was no basis of comparison for crew-size effects. It was impossible to determine the total number of vessels of these types that entered U.S. waters (thus subject to reporting requirements) and therefore impossible to estimate the average frequency of spills or failures for all ships regardless of crew size. As a consequence, there was no baseline for comparison. In addition, the reliability of the data bases came into question. The PIRS file data on ITBs, for example, included inconsistent vessel identification numbers, making it difficult to determine whether the vessel name search was yielding all data for each vessel.

In a second trial, the committee attempted to derive a broader sample by searching the data bases by company name, using companies known to operate with small crews. It was learned, however, that the CASMAIN and

Lloyd's data bases cannot be searched reliably by company name. As an alternative, a committee task group made a manual search of the Lloyd's data base by looking up a sample range of ships operated by eight foreign-flag companies reported to use small crews. All of each operator's ships between 19,000 and 30,000 gross registered tons were selected (a total of 51 ships), and casualty data was retrieved from the data base by vessel name. Each vessel's length of service was used to compute the overall fleet incidence of casualties and accidents. The result, for a total of 448 ship-years, was only 13 reported accidents, an average annual rate of 0.0266 per ship.

Again, as with the results summarized above for ships known to operate with small crews, there is no basis for comparison with larger crewed vessels. Furthermore, the result is an order of magnitude smaller than that obtained from the analysis of individual ships, suggesting that selection by fleet may introduce vessels that are out of service during some of the reporting period or that casualty reporting outside U.S. waters is less reliable.

Thus, the committee could not conduct a complete statistical analysis of the effect of vessel manning on safety performance. Existing U.S. and international maritime operations data are simply insufficient for deriving valid statistics about the safety of smaller crews. Further research in this area, supported by improved record-keeping worldwide, is essential.

Improving the Collection of Data

At present, the most comprehensive and detailed data on the safety of vessels with smaller crews is in the files of individual companies. All U.S.-flag operators could be asked to submit, on a confidential basis, whatever safety-related comparisons they maintain internally on their own vessels. Comparison and analysis of the safety indices used by different companies could then be undertaken, which would provide meaningful insights into current safety trends and additional factors that should be monitored.

Out of such a review should come recommendations as to how present Coast Guard reporting requirements should be modified to include factors that help identify meaningful relationships between casualties and injuries, on the one hand, and possible causal factors (e.g., vessel age, vessel size, crew size, crew overtime, crew continuity, and vessel equipment) on the other.

To make the most of its own data, the Coast Guard should revise its casualty and oil spill data bases to make them readily accessible for search information on the sizes and organizations of crews.

INDUSTRY SAFETY INFORMATION

In general, as noted earlier, the broad industry-wide data contain no direct information on the crew levels of vessels involved in accidents. However, such data, collected consistently over the past few decades, are meaningful, since crew sizes have been substantially reduced during this time. Thus, these data may offer some general insight into the safety implications of smaller crews. This insight is clouded, however, by other developments over the same period, such as more stringent requirements for safety equipment and procedures.

Though there are some variances, the available industry safety statistics indicate the following:

• There has been a measurable and substantial improvement in the rate of both vessel casualties (accidents) and personnel injuries during the past 20 years. More specifically, there has been a declining rate of vessel casualties, a declining rate of vessel losses as a result of accidents, and a declining rate of personnel injuries. These trends are evident on a nondimensional basis (e.g., percentage of total vessels, percentage of total gross tonnage, incidents per ship, and injuries per seagoing employee), that is, as a result of a methodology that eliminates the impact of changes in fleet size, numbers of employees, and other variables. These trends are consistent whether one considers statistics published by the International Maritime Organization (IMO) of the United Nations, by Lloyd's Casualty Reports, by the Marine Index Bureau, or by the U.S. Coast Guard.

• During the same 20-year period, the average crew size has declined substantially (from the low thirties to the low twenties for U.S.-flag vessels and to the high teens for many foreign fleets).

• While these two trends have occurred during the same time period, other factors have also changed. Technology has improved, operating procedures have been refined, and the scrutiny of maritime operations by government and industry bodies has increased. The safety data available from the various worldwide sources is not sufficiently detailed to correlate vessel casualties and personnel injuries with crew size. It is therefore not possible to isolate the effect of crew size to determine whether any causal relation, positive or negative, exists between crew size and safety. Neither is it possible to determine from the available data whether crew size, in itself, interacts with other variables to enhance or reduce safety.

Lloyd's Vessel Loss Data

Figure 2-1 displays worldwide total vessel loss rates over the past 20 years. During this period, the loss rate has dropped from about 0.65 percent to 0.32 percent per year—a 50 percent decline. Although total losses worldwide are a gross measure covering large and small vessels (individual years aside), the figure demonstrates that the combined impact of all factors—including changes in the size and types of vessels sailing, ship design, manning, and operating practices—has been to reduce total vessel losses substantially. In terms of tonnage (a more accurate indicator of commercial activity), a down trend is also evident (Figure 2-2). Although there was an upturn in the late 1970s, over the past 20 years annual tonnage losses have declined 20 percent, from about 0.35 percent to 0.28 percent per year.

Total losses of U.S.-flag vessels have also declined (Figure 2-3). The total loss percentage declined from about 0.4 percent in the early 1970s to about 0.10 percent recently, a figure only one-third the world average given in Figure 2-1. Figure 2-4 shows no trend in U.S.-flag percent tonnage loss, but the average, about 0.17 percent, is only about two-thirds of the world average shown in Figure 2-2. The considerable year-to-year variance in the U.S. figures is due to the small number of data points and the influence of large vessels (e.g., the *Manhattan* in 1987) on tonnage percentages. Nonetheless, the lower U.S. loss ratios indicate that some factors are keeping U.S.-flag vessels ahead of the world in preventing total losses of vessels. These factors may include the types of vessels under the U.S. flag, the trade routes served, U.S. Coast Guard and American Bureau of Shipping requirements, and the quality of American seamen.

Marine Index Bureau Injury Data

Statistical data on injuries are issued annually by the Marine Index Bureau. Figure 2-5 shows that, over the past 20 years, the aggregate incidence of injuries per working seaman in U.S. deepwater vessels has declined by more than 40 percent, from about 0.45 to 0.25 injuries per year per seagoing employee. While this is a gross aggregation of data, it supports a conclusion that during the last two decades the net impact of the aggregate changes in the seagoing environment has been to reduce injury rates for seamen significantly.

Tanker Casualty Data

A subset of total vessel data is tanker data developed by the International Maritime Organization (IMO). These data cover tankers not in layup or storage and over 6,000 gross tons. Figure 2-6 shows that, after rising in the late 1970s, worldwide casualty rates of large tank vessels have declined to about 2.0 per hundred vessels, a level roughly 20 percent below those of the mid to late 1970s.

The decline in the number of tankers lost (excluding war damage) is

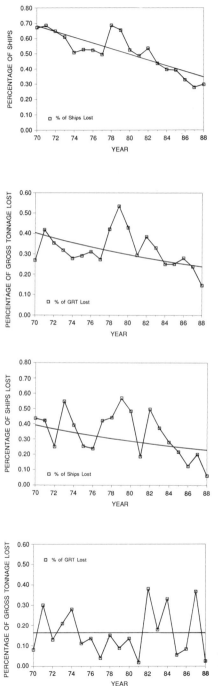

FIGURE 2-1 Worldwide vessel loss rates (percentage of ships) for commercial ships, 1970-1988. The decline in the percentage loss of commercial ships since 1970 has been linear at a confidence level exceeding 99 percent. Source: Data from Lloyd's Casualty Reports.

FIGURE 2-2 Worldwide vessel loss rates (percentage of gross tonnage) for commercial ships, 1970-1988. The decline in the rate of loss of commercial tonnage since 1970 has been nonlinear (power function) at a confidence level exceeding 99 percent. Source: Data from Lloyd's Casualty Reports.

FIGURE 2-3 Total loss rates of U.S.-flag vessels, 1970-1988 (percentages of vessels). The decline in the rate of loss of U.S.-flag inspected vessels since 1970 has been nonlinear (power function) at a confidence level exceeding 90 percent. Source: Data from Lloyd's Casualty Reports.

FIGURE 2-4 Total loss rates of U.S.-flag vessels, 1970-1988 (percentages of gross tonnage). The variation in the rate of loss of tonnage for U.S.-flag inspected vessels has exhibited a random behavior since 1970, which is best represented by an average value. Source: Data from Lloyd's Casualty Reports.

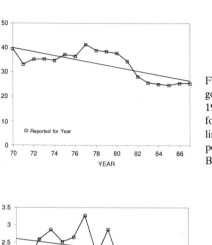

FIGURE 2-5 Annual injury rates per sea-going employee in U.S. deepwater vessels, 1970-1987. The decline in the injury rate for oceangoing seamen since 1970 has been linear at a confidence level exceeding 99 percent. Source: Data from Marine Index Bureau.

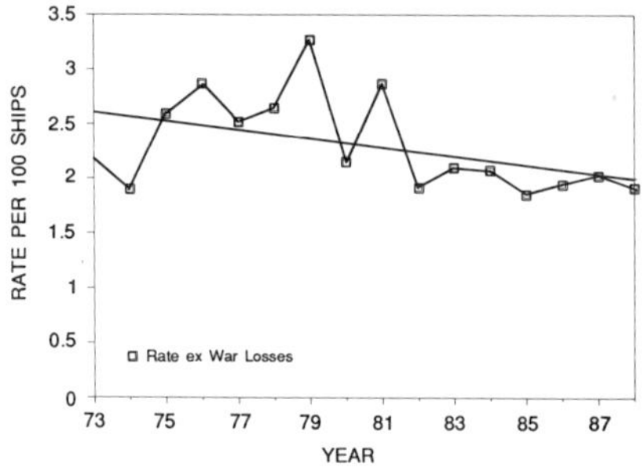

FIGURE 2-6 Rates of serious casualties of oil tankers (actively trading vessels over 6,000 gross tons), 1974-1988. The decline in the rate of serious tanker casualties since 1970 has been linear at a confidence level exceeding 90 percent. Source: Data from International Maritime Organization.

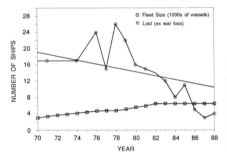

FIGURE 2-7 Numbers of tankers lost worldwide (excluding war damage), 1970-1988. The decline in the rate of loss of tankers worldwide since 1970 has been linear at a confidence level exceeding 90 percent. Source: Data from International Maritime Organization.

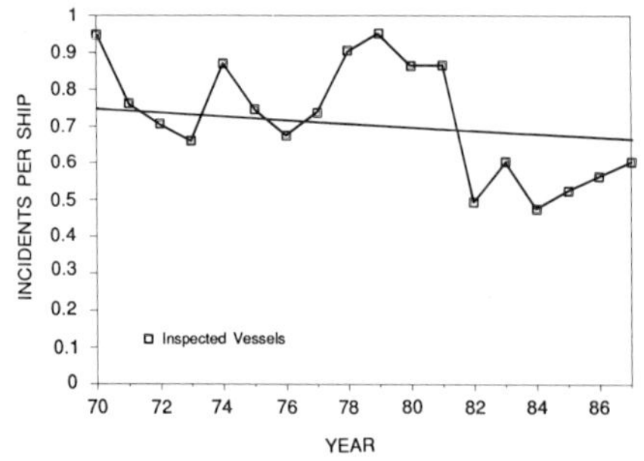

FIGURE 2-8 Reportable casualty rates of U.S.-flag ships, 1970-1986. Although there is a clear declining trend in the rate of casualties for U.S.-flag inspected vessels, the best estimation (nonlinear) correlates at a confidence level of less than 80 percent. Source: Data from U.S. Coast Guard, Annual Statistical Summary.

even more striking, as shown in Figure 2-7. Peaks occurred in the late 1970s, but total losses have since declined to half the prior levels, perhaps indicating that safety measures adopted by IMO (such as requirements for flooding crude tankers' tanks with inert gas) are having the desired effect.

U.S. Coast Guard Annual Casualty Reports

Information has also been developed from the Coast Guard's Annual Statistical Summary of casualties and personnel injuries on inspected U.S.-flag commercial vessels. Based on these data, reportable casualties per ship have declined from about 0.8 incidents per vessel per year in the early 1970s to 0.6 recently (Figure 2-8). Tanker incidents per vessel (Figure 2-9) seem to have held fairly constant in the 1.0 per ship per year range, with yearly variations as high as 1.4 and as low as 0.8. Correlated to tonnage, however, marked declines of over 20 percent for all vessels and 50 percent for tankers have occurred (Figure 2-10).

Oil Spill Data

U.S. Coast Guard data for 1975 through 1989 were reviewed for ascertainable trends. Figure 2-11 shows that the absolute number of reported oil spills from barges, tankers, and all vessels has been declining. The number of barge spills exceeds tanker spills every year.

Spills from vessels have also been declining as a percentage of total spills into water, which have also been declining (Figure 2-12). However, this favorable trend is not reflected in the data on volumes spilled. Figure 2-13 shows that spill volumes may vary greatly from year to year and have not changed greatly during the period reviewed. In this regard, note that, although barge spills are usually small, in 8 of 12 years the total volume spilled from barges exceeded the volume spilled from tankers. In addition, large tanker spills may double or triple the volume of oil spilled from vessels in a year. When such large spills occur, vessels account for upwards of 75 percent of oil spilled from all sources, compared with about 35 percent in nonpeak years. Thus, while emphasis on oil spill prevention may have reduced the number of spills in recent years, the total volume spilled in any year fluctuates greatly.

Individual Company Data

The committee was able to obtain some safety data from individual operators that have reduced their crews. Figure 2-14 shows trends in the number of billets, casualties, material failures and breakdowns, and personnel injuries and fatalities per ship for Company A during three-year

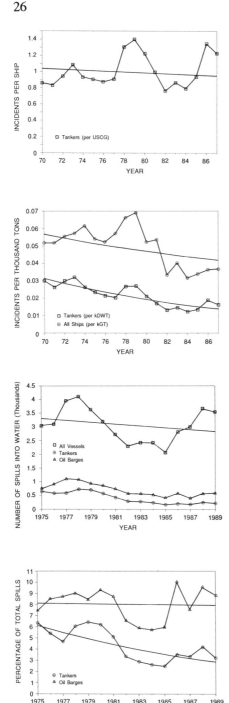

FIGURE 2-9   Reportable casualty rates of U.S.-flag tank ships, 1970-1986. Although there is a clear declining trend in the rate of casualties for U.S.-flag tankers, the best estimation (nonlinear) correlates at a confidence level of less than 80 percent. Source: Data from U.S. Coast Guard, Annual Statistical Summary.

FIGURE 2-10   Reportable casualty rates of U.S.-flag ships per thousand gross tons (upper curve), and U.S.-flag tank ships per thousand deadweight tons (lower curve), 1970-1986. In contrast to the low confidence in the correlation of the decline in casualties to the numbers of U.S.-flag commercial ships and tankers (Figures 2-8 and 2-9), the correlation to tonnage is very strong. For all vessels, the decline has been nonlinear (power function) at a confidence level exceeding 90 percent; for tankers, it has been exponential at a confidence level exceeding 99 percent. Source: Data from U.S. Coast Guard, Annual Statistical Summary.

FIGURE 2-11   Number of reported oil spills from (□) all vessels, (○) tankers, and (△) oil barges, 1975-1989. Data for 1987-1989 are preliminary only and should be used with caution. Although there appears to be a declining trend for the rate of oil spills by all vessels, the best estimate for this trend correlates at a confidence level of less than 80 percent. Source: Data from U.S. Coast Guard.

FIGURE 2-12   Percentages of total reported oil spills from tankers and oil barges, 1975-1989. Data for 1987-1989 are preliminary only and should be used with caution. The variation in the percentages for barges has been essentially random and is best represented as an average value equal to 8.02 percent. In contrast, the exponential decline in the percentage of spills from tankers correlates at a confidence level exceeding 99 percent. Source: Data from U.S. Coast Guard.

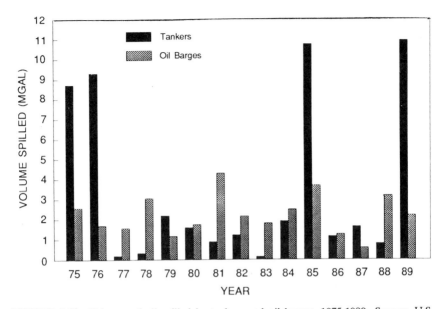

FIGURE 2-13 Volumes of oil spilled by tankers and oil barges, 1975-1989. Source: U.S. Coast Guard.

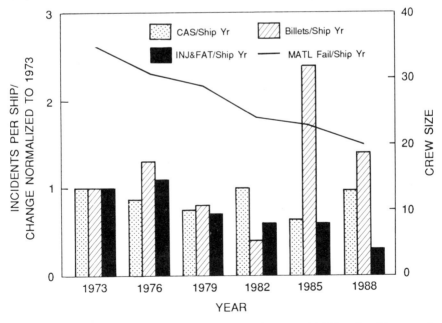

FIGURE 2-14 Trends in numbers of billets, casualties, material failures/breakdowns and personnel injuries/fatalities per ship for Company A during consecutive three-year intervals from 1973 to 1988 (indexed with 1973 = 1.0). Source: Marine Board Survey.

intervals from 1973 to 1988. While injuries and fatalities have declined as manning dropped, ship casualties fluctuated around an average of 0.53 per ship year.[1]

Data provided by Company B show marked declines in oil spills per vessel and personnel injuries per million man-hours worked (Figures 2-15 and 2-16). Oil spills per vessel have declined 45 percent in the last 15 years, and injuries per million man-hours worked have declined 50 percent. Since, as shown, the average number of employees per vessel in Company B has declined 30 percent (from 30 to 21) the absolute number of injuries per vessel has dropped 65 percent during the 15-year period.

Another large operator provided personnel injury data on 16 company ships whose crews were reduced from 34 to 21 people. Average annual injury rates per crew member during the three years following the change were virtually the same as the three previous years.

Safety Implications of Available Data

The historical data, viewed from several perspectives, show that the rates of vessel casualties and personnel injuries have improved over the past two decades. These improvements have occurred simultaneously with a significant reduction in the average crew size. However, no direct link has been detected between crew size and vessel or personnel safety. The broad statistics should not be considered a basis for complacency. The limited data from individual companies show that safety records are not uniform, illustrating the truism that safety must be addressed by each company in terms of its specific operations. Except for those from Company A and Company B, none of the data discussed above provide specific information on manning practices. The data's importance stems from the known steady decline in average vessel manning, approaching 50 percent since World War II, due to the introduction of newer, more automated vessels with smaller crews and to manpower reductions on existing vessels.

Some U.S.-flag ships have manning levels as low as 15 persons, while others have 25 or more. The larger crews are often on older vessels whose owners may not be convinced of the desirability of such automation or the certainty of payout on the required investment during the remaining life of the vessel.

Replacements for older vessels invariably have more automation and lower required manning, so the trend toward lower *average* manning will continue. Foreign companies operate vessels with as few as 8 to 12 people.

---

[1] The data on material failure in the figure represent days lost as the result of mechanical breakdowns.

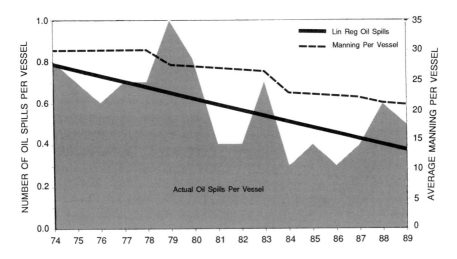

FIGURE 2-15 Manning levels and annual rates of oil spills per vessel, Company B, 1974-1989. The solid line is a linear regression fit to the data.

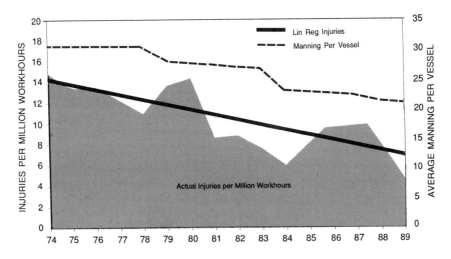

FIGURE 2-16 Manning levels and annual rates of personnel injuries per million work-hours, Company B, 1974-1989. The solid line is a linear regression fit to the data.

If they continue to operate safely, pressures will rise for the United States to follow suit.

SAFETY CONCERNS

Gross measures of performance provide few clues as to specific steps required to improve safety while further reducing manning. Safety factors and problems are best identified by the personnel involved, the licensed and unlicensed people working aboard the vessels, and the owners and operators. Accordingly, committee members and staff visited with unions and vessel operators to obtain their opinions and verify their concerns.

Labor Organizations

The committee solicited the views of maritime labor organizations representing licensed and unlicensed personnel serving aboard U.S.-flag vessels. At the committee meeting of September 13-15, 1989, spokesmen for 10 labor organizations described their safety experiences and concerns. Many also submitted written statements and other documents. Appendix C lists these spokesmen and the materials they submitted.

Many union representatives believe safety has deteriorated with smaller crews. They point to increased fatigue due to longer working hours, poor maintenance practices, and fewer opportunities for on-the-job training. Some express a lack of confidence in the Coast Guard's even-handedness in addressing labor-management issues (Alliance of Independent Maritime Organizations, 1989; Hillman, 1989; International Transport Workers Federation, 1990).

Vessel Operators

The committee members and staff visited the offices of nine U.S.-owned vessel operators to conduct interviews (see Appendix D for questionnaire), and toured one vessel. The companies operate tank ships, tug-barge combinations, bulk carriers, container ships, and special purpose ships, under both U.S. and foreign flags. Some, such as major oil companies, own their own ships, carry their own products, and hire their own crews. Others manage for other owners and hire from union rosters.

Operators generally believe safety has improved aboard ships with smaller crews, owing to greater safety consciousness and improved equipment. They point out that crew reductions require better trained personnel who are able to accept more responsibility and to manage automated systems. Recognizing that elimination of most entry-level positions has reduced opportunities for on-the-job training, they believe they are taking steps to ensure the necessary competence and thereby maintain or improve safety.

Some operators cited fatigue and the difficulty of retaining key personnel (especially junior licensed officers) as management challenges resulting from moves toward smaller crews. Most have made changes in maintenance practices to relieve crew members of some of their workload.

Specific Safety Concerns

More important than the general opinions expressed by labor and operators was the fact that they identified many common safety concerns. These concerns should be the object of efforts to further improve safety.

Fatigue

The potential for fatigue is the safety concern voiced most often and is taken seriously by labor and management. Both recognize that inattention can cause accidents. A few casualties have been attributed to inattention associated with fatigue. The recent *World Prodigy* grounding and oil spill near Newport, Rhode Island, is an example (National Transportation Safety Board, 1989).

Coast Guard casualty reports rarely note fatigue as a contributing factor; however, there is reason to believe that its contribution is under-reported, owing to reporting procedures (Pettin, 1987). Complicating analysis of the problem is the difficulty of measuring fatigue. Hours worked is at best a rough indicator, one which does not measure stress, the nature of the work performed, or the physical condition of the employee (Pollard, 1990).

Long working hours are common in the maritime industry, and indeed desired by many union members as a means of increasing their take-home pay. Since shipboard workers do not commute or cook their own meals, long hours may not be as tiring as they would be ashore. Where long hours are a recognized problem (e.g., the round-the-clock cargo responsibilities of deck officers or the heavy workloads imposed by frequent port calls), many companies employ personnel in excess of the minimums set by the Coast Guard to compensate for the increased work load. Others use shore-based personnel for cargo operations, so that crew members may rest.

Little information is available to indicate the increase or decrease in working hours as crews have been reduced. Although some companies indicate that overtime has not changed significantly, some labor organizations are genuinely concerned that smaller crews mean more hours worked, more fatigue for remaining licensed and unlicensed personnel, and therefore degradation of safety. Management responds by saying that, properly managed, average working hours need not increase and that in some cases fatigue may decrease; for example, in engine rooms certified for unmanned operation, engine department personnel can work days only instead of standing four-hour on, eight-hour off watches. In a given situation, either point of view may be correct, depending on the degree of work planning and management of work effort.

Maintenance Practices

Traditionally, vessel crews have done most routine deck and engine maintenance. Newer materials and design changes have eliminated some of this work or made it a biennial shipyard repair item. Nonetheless, ship safety will be impaired if reduced manning causes deferral of needed maintenance on safety-related equipment.

Union representatives have filed grievances alleging that crew reductions have resulted in essential safety equipment being allowed to remain in disrepair in violation of Coast Guard regulations and collective bargaining agreements (Hillman, 1989). Coast Guard personnel also have blamed crew reductions for maintenance deficiencies. In reporting a 1988 incident involving the simultaneous failure of electrical power and propulsion systems on a ship near the harbor entrance at Portland, Maine, the commander of the First Coast Guard District pointed out that the vessel's reduced engineering complement made adequate maintenance "impossible" (Folsom, 1988). Furthermore, he stated, "Shoreside or riding maintenance crews look good on paper but are easily dropped, especially considering the economic conditions that currently plague the U.S. fleet." He expressed the opinion that "revalidation of reduced manning levels should be occurring with every Inspection for Certification." He noted that many chief engineers favor the licensing of electronics engineers to maintain automated systems.

To avoid this potential problem while carrying smaller crews, some companies employ "riding crews" or repair firms to perform needed maintenance in port. These approaches may be quite acceptable, but it remains incumbent on the companies to maintain records demonstrating compliance with Coast Guard regulations.

Emergency Response Capacity

Operators and unions agree that more attention to safety systems and emergency procedures will be necessary as crews are further reduced.

Three general categories of emergency should be considered:

• First—and perhaps most critical—is the "all hands" type, such as fire and explosion, collision, or grounding. Vessel design and personnel training can help ensure the shipboard capability to evaluate and respond.

Preventive maintenance programs can help ensure that the vessel is in condition to operate properly and safely. Strict adherence to safety procedures (e.g., the use of fireproof doors in cargo areas) is also necessary. (Chapter 4 discusses a modeling exercise in which the personnel requirements for fighting an engine room fire are calculated.)

• Second, the vessel must be able to operate safely in case of power losses and failures of vital equipment such as steering gear, navigational equipment, mooring equipment, the main propulsion plant (including loss of automation and problems with diesel engines or boilers), and cargo gear.

• Third is the ability to handle personnel casualties. Manning decisions must allow rapid and efficient response without depriving the vessel of its ability to operate. For example, evacuating a crew member by helicopter requires enough personnel to transfer the injured person (including at least four stretcher bearers) as well as enough to operate the ship. Rescues at sea presently involve at least six people in addition to those left aboard to operate the ship. Launching and retrieving lifeboats also can be labor intensive.

Some operators and labor representatives interviewed stressed the importance of redundant safety systems (including internal communications equipment) capable of operation from several places on the vessel.

Reduced Training Opportunities for Unlicensed Personnel

The elimination of entry-level positions (such as wiper and ordinary seaman) on many vessels has reduced the opportunity for on-the-job training, some of which is required for the more responsible positions that remain such as oiler and able-bodied seaman. Both labor and management personnel agreed that inexperienced or inadequately trained personnel can create safety problems, whether on watch, handling cargo, or operating emergency and safety systems.

To prevent such problems, some companies have instituted "cadet" programs to train unlicensed personnel. Others hire in excess of the normal complement until crew members gain the necessary experience. Recent high unemployment in shipping has allowed some companies to meet their skill requirements by recruiting recent graduates of maritime academies (who are licensed officers) to work in unlicensed positions; the industry's expected upturn may limit that option. A few companies in recent years have negotiated labor contracts that provide for employment continuity among key personnel, thus ensuring that investments in additional training can be recaptured (see, for example, American President Lines, 1989). Whatever the approach, it is essential that Coast Guard certifications be based on demonstrated proficiency and that management exercise diligence to promote or hire only qualified people.

Service Continuity by Crew Members

All operators agreed that continuity of service by crew members is an important safety factor, particularly with sophisticated shipboard systems requiring intimate knowledge. Repeated service aboard the same vessel ensures familiarity with the equipment and promotes teamwork. Continuity is most desirable among key personnel (master, chief engineer, chief mate, and 1st assistant engineer), and is helpful with junior officers and unlicensed personnel as well. One operator noted that crew levels of 9 to 11 would require 100 percent continuity.

Physical Demands on Crew Members

Concerns were also expressed about the growing need for physical fitness of crew members. Smaller crews mean fewer people available for emergency operations and very likely fewer physically strong people in situations where strength is needed. Assessments of minimum manning levels must take into account the degree to which labor-saving devices are available or tasks requiring strength have been eliminated.

Several of those interviewed pointed out the desirability of designing vessels to minimize things such as unnecessary ladder climbing or heavy lifting to eliminate some of the causes of injuries as well as impediments to emergency response. Annual physical examinations were recommended by some operators. To be effective in improving safety more rigid standards of "fitness for duty" may need to be established and enforced.

Changed Shipboard Social Conditions

Recognizing that attitudes may affect alertness and attention to safety rules, several operators expressed concern over the impact of reduced manning on the shipboard social environment. With the smaller licensed and unlicensed groups and the breakdown of some of the traditional distinctions between the deck, engine, and steward's departments, new social structures will be necessary. Some companies are already promoting the ship's team concept, an effort that may be assisted by movement toward greater continuity of assignments. One operator, whose ships carry crews as small as 14 persons, reported that it had used psychologists from the beginning of its manpower reduction program.

FURTHER RESEARCH

Better information is needed on the relationship between crew size and safety experience. As noted earlier, the Coast Guard data bases are presently inadequate to support even retrospective conclusions about the safety records of U.S.-flag vessels that have reduced crews. Prospective regulatory judgments to support further reductions of crews rest on an even more inadequate base since the Coast Guard has not developed the human factors methods to assess such steps.

In addition to the broad safety statistics, more detailed safety studies of the following factors are needed to support the manning innovations now being undertaken or contemplated by U.S.-flag fleets. Such studies should consider the following:

- the prevalence and severity of fatigue aboard merchant ships, with attention to the role of fatigue in navigation errors and personnel accidents;
- the human factors issues presented by the one-person bridge, including the operators' responses to fatigue and the ergonomic design of control and monitoring systems;
- changes in maintenance practices owing to reductions in engineering complements;
- the maintenance effectiveness of riding crews and shore-based maintenance;
- the effects of traditional watch schedules on crew members' circadian rhythms, and the consequent impacts on effectiveness and safety; and
- the data collection requirements for adequate assessments of the safety effects of smaller crews.

FINDINGS

Rates of maritime casualties and personnel injuries, worldwide and in the U.S.-flag fleet, have declined steadily over the last two decades, at the same time that the manning of vessels has been reduced. While concerns about safety have been raised—including neglected maintenance, increased fatigue and stress, and lessened opportunities for on-the-job training—management, labor unions, and governments have addressed these concerns through training, qualification standards, and other management techniques. The committee did not find in its analysis of safety data or its contacts with industry and labor in the United States and worldwide any direct causal relationships between vessel manning levels and safety.

Currently available maritime safety information is inadequate for making definite judgments about the contributions of various factors to maritime safety. While good information exists concerning numbers of casualties and the extent of damage, it is difficult to assemble information needed to calculate frequency of occurrence and assign the frequencies to different populations of ships (type, flag and age of ship, and numbers of crew). This information is needed to establish trends and make decisions about safety. Information about the causes of casualties is also not uniformly assembled.

Information on the prospective consequences of further reductions, which may involve substantial reorganizations of manning patterns, is also insufficient for firm judgments. The human factors studies to support increasing automation, for example, are only now beginning to appear, mainly in Europe.

REFERENCES

Alliance of Independent Maritime Organizations. 1989. The invasion of the sixty hour workweek standard and manning reductions in the U.S. Maritime Industry. Statement Submitted to the Committee on the Effect of Smaller Crews on Maritime Safety, National Research Council, Washington, D.C. September 14.

American President Lines. 1989. Marine Operations Department training program 1990. Mimeo. Oakland, California.

Commission on Merchant Marine and Defense. 1988. Third Report of the Commission on Merchant Marine and Defense. Washington, D.C.: U.S. Government Printing Office. Sept. 30.

Folsom, D. L. 1988. Vessel automation control reliability, reduced manning, maintenance, and operator responsibility. Memorandum from Commander, First Coast Guard District, to Chief, Office of Marine Safety, Security and Environmental Protection, U.S. Coast Guard. Dec. 19.

Hillman, John L. 1989. Letter from President, Exxon Seaman's Union, to Charles Bookman, Executive Director, Marine Board, National Research Council. September 21.

International Transport Workers' Federation. 1990. Submission to the Eighth Session of the ILO/IMO Joint Committee on Training (JCT8), Geneva, 17-21, September.

Meade, N.F., R.C. Anderson, N.J. Goldberg, V.F. Keith, and R.M. Willis. 1981. An analysis of tanker casualties for the ten year period, 1969-1978. *In* Proceedings of the 1981 Oil Spill Prevention Conference. Washington, D.C.: Courtesy Associates.

National Transportation Safety Board. 1989. Hearing record, joint NTSB-U.S. Coast Guard Marine Board of Investigation examination of Capt. Iakovas Georgoudis in the matter of the M/T *World Prodigy* grounding in Rhode Island Sound on June 23, 1989. Oct. 3.

Perkins, M. R. 1988. Vessel automation control reliability, reduced manning, maintenance, and operator responsibility: First endorsement on MSO Portland's ltr 16711 of 6 Dec 88. Memorandum from Commanding Officer, Marine Safety Office, Portland, Maine, to Commandant, U.S. Coast Guard.

Pettin, Thomas J. 1987. Fatigue as the cause of marine accidents, 1981-1985. U.S. Coast Guard, Marine Investigation Division. March.

Pollard, J.K., M. Sterns, and E. D. Sussman. 1990. Shipboard Crew Fatigue, Safety, and Reduced Manning. Contract report for Office of Technology Assessment and U.S. Maritime Administration. (Transportation Systems Center, Research and Special Programs Administration, Cambridge MA 02142).

Ponce, Paul V. 1990. An analysis of marine total losses worldwide and for selected flags. Marine Technology 27(2):114-116. March.

3
Managing the Human Factors
Aspects of Change

The introduction of new technology in ships sometimes permits reductions of crew sizes. However, these changes must be well thought out and tested extensively before full implementation. Ships are complex sociotechnical systems, consisting of (1) technologies, (2) people, (3) organizational structures, and (4) an external environment. As the literature on sociotechnical systems shows, the four dimensions are interdependent; when one changes, it affects the other three. Because of this fundamental interdependence, the introduction of technological change can not be viewed in isolation, or even at a subsystem level; it must be viewed from a true systems perspective. Thus, whether the introduction of new technology will permit safe reduction in manning will depend on whether appropriate changes can be made in the other three sociotechnical system dimensions. If inappropriate changes are made, or if the macrosystem in which the ship system is enmeshed constrains appropriate changes, then simply reducing crew size is likely to have unintended or undesirable effects that result in a reduction in safety. Undesirable human factors effects are especially likely under these circumstances (e.g., see DeGreene, 1973).

The sociotechnical systems literature has shown that where change to all four sociotechnical system dimensions can be properly managed, the introduction of new technology can not only increase productivity, but also improve working conditions, the intrinsic motivational features of jobs, and safety. In short, proper introduction of technology using a true systems approach provides an opportunity to improve health, safety, the quality of work life, and operating efficiency.

37

In the case of ships, stress, fatigue, boredom, living/social conditions, and individual and team skills are among the most critical human factors issues that must be addressed in managing the introduction of technological change from a systems perspective. Adoption of new technology will need to be supported by training, reallocations of personnel responsibilities, and careful attention to ergonomic design.

HUMAN FACTORS REQUIRING PARTICULAR ATTENTION

The extent to which technology implementation and associated crew reductions increase the risks of stress, fatigue, and boredom is not precisely known, since little research has been devoted to stress in the shipboard environment. Relatively high levels of stress and fatigue are considered normal in the maritime world. However, anecdotal evidence and the results of the few studies carried out aboard ship tend to confirm the conclusions one might draw from studies in the laboratory and in other working environments, such as aircraft and long-distance trucks (Hockey, 1986; Parasuraman, 1986, 1987). These sources suggest that stress, fatigue, and boredom, if not appropriately addressed, may be significant safety concerns aboard ship.

It should be noted that feelings of stress and fatigue, as well as degraded human performance, may result from either too high or too low a workload (Saunders and McCormick, 1988; Salvendy, 1987). Jobs that are physically or mentally demanding can produce erratic performance and/or narrowing of attention. Too light a workload—most likely to occur in passive monitoring tasks, with infrequent stimuli that require active response—can result in a low level of arousal of the central nervous system, with an attendant lack of vigilance and feelings of boredom and sleepiness (Hockey, 1986; Thackray, 1987).

These concerns suggest the need for caution and the need for further crew reductions to be based on sound research conducted under realistic conditions with a thorough analysis of the human factors issues involved.

Work Hours and Fatigue

There are no universally accepted standards defining maximum or permissible work hours for shipboard personnel. Some European national authorities do have written standards setting work hour limitations for vessels in their national fleets (International Transport Workers' Federation, 1990). However, U.S. maritime statutes do not contain meaningful guidance or standards for defining permissible work hours.

If smaller crews mean longer working hours, the result may be increased fatigue. Fatigue may show up as lack of attention during or after peak periods and could cause accidents, endangering life or property. The round-the-clock responsibilities of deck officers during cargo operations are of special concern, since ships may leave port after loading under the guidance of severely fatigued officers.

Other crew members may suffer similarly from disrupted sleep and associated fatigue. Vessels that make frequent port calls are of special concern, since crew members must interrupt their sleep often for mooring, unmooring, and cargo operations. Beetham (1989) notes, "Certain classes of ship, notably coastal, gas and chemical tankers, make particularly heavy demands upon their crew, which can give rise to serious fatigue. This should be taken into account by the flag state when issuing their manning certificates."

A study by the Coast Guard's Marine Investigation Division found that, between 1981 and 1985, fatigue was listed as a direct or indirect cause of casualties in only about 1 vessel in every 200 involved (Pettin, 1987). However, the author noted, "It is believed that the impact of fatigue in casualties is substantially under reported as most accidents are not investigated in sufficient detail to identify its exact role" (Pettin, 1987).

Some of the tendency for working hours to increase is mitigated, in some companies' fleets, by efforts to shift maintenance activities to shore personnel or to special "riding crews" that are carried aboard ships to perform maintenance. These shifts may produce their own risks; however, where safety-related maintenance is deferred, some regulators and others have noted a deterioration of maintenance standards associated with smaller crews (Folsom, 1988; Perkins, 1988). In any case, these organizational changes have little effect on the most critical fatigue-related risk, that of deck officers' inattention on the bridge.

Organizational innovations developed in Japan and Western Europe could help alleviate some acute fatigue at peak work periods by spreading the work load more evenly among crew members. For example, a few nations license dual-qualified officers, able to work in both engine and deck capacities. More common is the use of general purpose ratings, similarly able to cross departmental lines. In this country, so far, the nearest approach to such flexibility is the certification of some vessels to carry maintenance departments, composed of nonwatch-keeping personnel who perform maintenance, but can also be assigned to help in the engine or deck department as needed.

Moves to increase work flexibility across traditional departmental lines with general purpose unlicensed ratings and dual-qualified officers have not met with broad acceptance in the United States. The U.S. Merchant Marine Academy at Kings Point, New York, in the past has offered students the opportunity for dual licenses in both deck and engine specialties, but these intensive programs have attracted fewer and fewer enrollees, largely because young officers are encouraged to specialize by the departmental distinctions built into manning statutes and the license structure, accumulating the necessary hours of service on deck or in the engine room to qualify for the next steps in their licenses.

The academy today is instituting a pilot program with the intent of qualifying ship operations officers for newer, more automated ships, in which control functions are being centralized on the bridge. In these circumstances, watch officers responsible for operating engines as well as navigating will need greater training in engine operations (personal communication, Paul Krinsky, Superintendent, U.S. Maritime Academy, November 15, 1989).

Standard Watch Rotations and Fatigue

The traditional watch schedule followed by most of the world's fleet, with four hours on and eight off, seems designed to interfere with normal sleep cycles. Some researchers have proposed alternatives. In the laboratory, sleep loss or sleep disruption lowers human performance in mental tasks involving working memory, and lengthens the response time to critical events. One important finding is that fatigue and sleep loss, like exposure to loud noises, heat, vibration, and other physical sources of stress, generally produce a narrowing, or selectivity, of attention. That is, in dual-source vigilance tasks (e.g., monitoring two indicators), subjects tend to monitor one source more closely than the other. They also tend to focus on the expected event, often missing the unexpected when it happens (Hockey, 1986).

In one of the few shipboard experiments to document fatigue effects related to sleep loss, a two-year study conducted on German vessels found that the standard three-watch system (four on, eight off) upsets crew members' circadian rhythms and deprives them of sleep (Low et al., 1987). Low and his colleagues confirmed that personnel do not fully adapt to night watches and are generally less alert then (see also Hockey, 1986). In addition, they found that the three-watch rotation imposes more measurable stress (as indicated by physiological measures such as catecholamine and electrolyte excretion rates) than two-watch systems. They recommend for general use a system in which each watch keeper has a 10- to 14-hour period of unbroken free time each day, to permit uninterrupted sleep.

Another shipboard study, funded by the West German Ministry for Technology and Research, confirmed that the three-watch system produces sleep disruption that degrades performance in monitoring and judgment, especially during the night (Colquhoun et al., 1988; Condon et al., 1988; Rutenfranz, 1988). The research group proposed a new system that would give the second and third officers full-length periods of unbroken sleep each day, by assigning them to 12-hour watches followed by 12 hours of free time (Fletcher et al., 1988).

This issue is not directly related to crew size, except to the extent that vessels with smaller crews may make heavier demands on crew members' time and stamina, aggravating any possible effects of fatigue.

The Impact of Automation

Highly automated ships with smaller crews will place new demands on crew members. When automation is poorly designed or crews inappropriately or inadequately trained, the result can be increased boredom, fatigue, and stress. The goal is to establish optimal levels of mental workload for each shipboard function that is to be automated.

Human factors concerns have received insufficient review in shipboard automation, as they have in most complex engineering systems. Many automated systems reduce operators to passive monitors (Parasuraman, 1987; Schuffel et al., 1989) and remove much of the active content from the job without decreasing the need for vigilance. In addition, some say, the lack of standardization and the poor ergonomics of the systems make them difficult and confusing to use. One pilot told the committee, "Computerized navigational systems are designed without obtaining input from the ultimate user. They do not use common language and nautical terms to define functions. As a result, the people serving on board ship must accommodate the manufacturer and learn the specific programs involved in the equipment, rather than the other way around. At some point vessel safety will be compromised" (Bobb, 1989).

Integrated Bridge Systems

The extent of these problems for operators of newer, state-of-the-art bridge automation systems is uncertain. The bridge, in some new ships, has become a ship operation center, incorporating controls and monitors for all essential vessel functions, including navigation, engine control, and communications. Many routine navigational tasks, such as chart updating, position plotting, and steering, may be automated. Ballast may be adjustable from the bridge while the ship is underway. Logs, reports, certificates, documents, and letters may be computerized, with electronic mail links via satellite to shore (Grove, 1989). When systems are working properly, this environment may be stimulating enough to keep the officer on the bridge awake and alert. On the other hand, it may be distracting enough to degrade performance on critical course-keeping and collision-avoidance tasks.

In most cases where integrated bridges are introduced, bridge equipment is automated and decision aids are added (Grabowski, 1989; Kristiansen et al., 1989; Schuffel et al., 1989). The systems need to be designed in a systems engineering fashion, with careful attention to the operator tasks to be supported, limitations of the hardware and software, appropriate allocation of tasks between humans and machines, and ergonomic and human factors design. However, decision aids that have been developed within the context of integrated bridge designs have often been stand-alone systems, not integrated with existing bridge designs (Grabowski, 1989).

The results of experiments evaluating the impact of integrated bridge systems on bridge watch team performance have been mixed. Kristiansen, Renswick, and Mathisen (1989) found improved track-keeping and watch-keeping skills in experiments aboard seven Norwegian ships outfitted with highly automated bridges equipped with decision aids. Grabowski (1989) described the piloting expert system, a navigation aid for pilots and ship's officers. In tests at MARAD'S Computer Aided Operations Research Facility (CAORF) ship simulator, junior watch officers using the aid showed improved watch-keeping skills, but showed no significant improvement in track-keeping. The system is one piece of an integrated bridge system. Unlike Schuffel's (1989) design, it is not intended to integrate all bridge functions and so cannot be judged on the basis of its allocation of functions between human and computer.

Single-Handed Bridge Operation

Single-handed bridges—on which the watch officer serves also as helmsman and lookout—are being introduced by some foreign-flag shipping operators, and some national certificating authorities have permitted some vessels to operate this way, provided they have certain automated equipment (Habberley, 1989; Vail, 1988). Many other vessels reportedly operate in this way without permission, even in restricted waters (Beetham, 1989; Habberley, 1989; Parker, 1987; George Quick, International Order of Masters, Mates and Pilots, oral statement at September 13, 1989, committee meeting).

One attempt to integrate bridge functions aboard single-handed bridges, with a careful allocation of functions between humans and computer, is described in a paper by Schuffel (1989). In a simulation study of navigation performance and mental workload, an officer of the watch focused on the feasibility of single-handed navigation using an automated bridge design called "Wheelhouse 90." He found that "a careful functional allocation [between human and computer] can lead to an automated wheelhouse concept suitable to single-handed navigation." His analysis of 276 accidents due to human error showed that 68 percent would have been prevented by a single-handed bridge similar to the one described in his paper. Schuffel notes, however, that "ship control tasks have changed from active manual control actions to passive monitoring activities," and he warns against such reductions of operators to passive monitors of control systems.

Kristiansen, Renswick, and Mathisen (1989) also studied single-handed bridge operations, and found watch officers generally satisfied with the bridge configuration, workload, and levels of stress, and with the absence of a lookout. Two essential elements of the officers' satisfaction were identified: (1) single-handed operations were restricted to times when the ships were in open seas under favorable environmental conditions, and (2) watch officers could suspend single-handed operations when necessary.

A two-year study by Low et al. (1987) of watch-keeping officers on 10 West German ships with single-handed bridges found different results. There were objective indications of stress and only partial adaptation of circadian cycles to night watches, even though officers generally kept the same watch cycle every day for months. The authors recommended adjusting watch rotations, carefully selecting personnel, and operating with two people on the bridge at all times.

Some empirical research shows that officers serving single-handed watches aboard such "Ship of the Future" bridges were significantly better at maintaining the vessel's course than traditional watches (Kristiansen et al., 1989; Schuffel et al., 1989). These improvements were reported to have been accomplished with no accompanying information overload. However, caution with single-handed bridges is wise, because this mode of operation places responsibility for the ship on a single fallible person. No one may be present to catch errors, to take over if the officer of the watch is incapacitated, or to help keep the officer of the watch awake. More empirical work assessing mental workload, required decision supports, and human-machine trade-offs needs to be done.

Deck and Engine Room Automation

The U.S. Coast Guard specifies the levels of automation in certain systems necessary for safe operation with reduced manning levels. Deck manning reductions are permitted if the vessel has adequate labor-saving equipment, such as automated (self-adjusting) mooring winches, automated hatch cover securing equipment, and internal communications equipment sufficient to raise reinforcements if necessary (U.S. Coast Guard, *Marine Safety Manual*, 23.A.2). Automated engine departments are subject to the restriction that the vessel carry the minimum crew to safeguard it if all automated systems fail, including enough personnel for round-the-clock watches (*Marine Safety Manual*, 23.A.3).

Organizational changes associated with reductions in engine room watch-standing and operating personnel have had a significant impact on combatting fatigue, boredom, and inattention. Unattended engine rooms relieve engineers of the traditional four-hour-on, eight-hour-off watches. Instead, automation and alarm systems provide surveillance previously provided by engine room watch-standers. The watch-standing engineers are thus organized into day working teams, working 8 a.m. to 5 p.m. shifts in groups, often troubleshooting problems together. One engineer is on call each night to respond to emergencies. The result has been increased socialization by the engineers, greater job satisfaction, and increased productivity. Interestingly, the deck officers aboard such ships—who were previously paired with their engine room watch-standing counterparts—have been increasingly alienated by these changes.

Sociological Impacts

Changes in shipboard living conditions due to the use of smaller crews (such as less social interaction and less time ashore) could produce a variety of stress reactions that make shipboard personnel less reliable. Some vessel operators regard this risk as serious and have assigned psychologists to address the problem in the course of manning reductions. On cargo vessels running experimentally with very small crews, scheduling pressures and minimal crew size means that shore leave is nearly nonexistent. On one Europe-to-North America run by a Swedish container ship, crew members stay aboard ship for the entire 28-day round-trip voyage in the company of as few as 15 shipmates, including officers.

Attempts to address the problem on smaller-crewed vessels include moves toward increased social integration of officers and crew and rearrangement of living and working spaces to encourage interaction. Most of these approaches have been pioneered in Europe and Japan, but a few U.S. operators are beginning to adopt some of them.

Drug and Alcohol Abuse

There is no evidence to suggest that drug and alcohol abuse has increased during the past 30 years while average crew size has fallen. However, the problems of shipboard drug and alcohol abuse could become more serious as crews grow smaller, since there would be fewer crew members to compensate for impaired shipmates.

The Coast Guard in late 1988 issued its final rule, "Programs for Chemical Testing of Commercial Vessel Personnel" (CGD 86-067), requiring employers to establish drug and alcohol control programs, including testing before employment, after accidents, and under other specified conditions (National Transportation Safety Board, 1989). Since mid-1989, each crew member has been required to possess a "drug-free certificate" when first joining a vessel. Regulations prohibit a crew member's standing watch if he or she has consumed any alcohol within the previous four hours. A person is considered legally intoxicated if his or her blood alcohol content is 0.04 percent or greater. Companies are now also required to have alcohol test kits on board, with personnel trained in their use, to test crew members suspected of being intoxicated.

Many companies have introduced programs to teach key shipboard personnel to detect alcohol or drug abusers. Some have established strict prohibitions on alcohol consumption aboard ship. Others limit alcohol consumption to the use of beer during restricted hours. Many companies and unions have formal drug and alcohol addiction treatment programs. In the future, companies may go further; personnel selection and assignment decisions, for example, may hinge on evidence of past drug or alcohol abuse.

Adequacy of Coast Guard Human Factors Analyses

The U.S. Coast Guard recognizes the need to use more sophisticated human factors tools in judging the adequacy of future manning levels. As vessels are further automated and crews grow smaller, this need will become greater. At present, the Coast Guard has no explicit human factors models for judging the risks of stress, fatigue, and boredom.

Automation of ships must address not only the reliability of the hardware and software (and its ability to fail safely, without endangering the vessel), but also the training requirements imposed by the automated system and the design of the human-computer interface to make it user-friendly. The design process is complex and subtle; the penalty for failure can be very high.

MANAGING THE HUMAN FACTORS ASPECTS OF CHANGE

As noted in this chapter, much additional human factors research is needed to clarify the human factors implications of technological change in the maritime industry. However, as suggested by research already accomplished, sufficient knowledge does exist to effectively manage the critical human factors issues noted. The additional research needs cited above will enable the maritime industry to more knowledgeably, effectively, and precisely manage change. Much can be done to address each of the major human factors issues within the present state of the art.

Fatigue and Boredom

While there is much still to be learned, it is known that excessively long work periods are likely to result in serious fatigue that can increase the likelihood of human error. As noted earlier, voyage profiles that call for frequent in-port time loading and unloading cargo and related transiting of restricted waters greatly increase the man hours worked. Any technological change that reduces shipboard manning will have to address the distribution of work load among crew members (and possibly shore-based personnel) and the organizational structure of the macrosystem to ensure that excessively long work periods do not occur. This systems assurance must be verified as a part of the authorization for reduced shipboard manning if safety is to be preserved. Function and task analysis methods can be adapted to assist in this purpose; a functional analysis model developed by this committee is described in Chapter 4.

Another factor known to increase the likelihood of fatigue is the traditional watch rotation system, which fails to provide a long rest period (10-14 hours) each day for uninterrupted sleep and relaxation. Use of a revised watch system on long voyages may reduce fatigue and could become an important component of operating safely with small crews.

It should be noted that the proper introduction of new technology not only may enable a reduction of crew size, but also may actually reduce the workload or other fatigue-inducing aspects of the job for the remaining crew members. An excellent example of this has been the development of the unattended engine room and elimination of watches for the engine personnel (described in Chapter 1 and later in this chapter).

New technology provides a unique opportunity to ergonomically re-design jobs and related human-machine interfaces to make them intrinsically more interesting. In particular, providing for active as well as passive activity and a sufficient variety of tasks is essential to minimizing boredom (and related subjective fatigue) and maintaining alertness. This type of good ergonomic design is within the state of the art for automated systems, and should be incorporated in any automated system's design process.

The redesign of jobs will require breaking away from the traditional departmental and officer-crew distinctions, which are based on old technologies. It also will increase the skill requirements of jobs, and hence their education and training requirements. Changes in regulations and union-management relationships and contracts are likely to be required to redesign these jobs and change related sociotechnical systems.

For tasks in which vigilance is critical, such as watch-keeping, the use of technological innovations such as integrated information and decision support systems should enhance reliability and safety. For single-handed navigation, the use of "dead man" switches and alarm systems to guard against lapses in attention, sleep, or sudden incapacitation are well within the state of the art. The key is to require these technological features and ensure that they are effective before authorizing single-handed bridge operation.

Excessive Workload

Careful attention to function and task analysis of jobs and equipment redesign can prevent excessive load on the worker. Such analysis of the design and implementation of new technology is well within the state of the art of ergonomics. It must be done using a systems approach, since careful distribution of work load among the crew becomes critical as crew size is reduced. The use of a shipboard maintenance department represents a first step in this direction. Chapter 4 describes a functional task analysis model developed by the committee, which could be used by operators and regulators to ensure the appropriate allocation of tasks aboard ship as new technology is adopted.

Shipboard Living Conditions

Careful ergonomic attention to the design of living areas can enhance living conditions and improve social interaction of crew members. With small crews, a breakdown of the traditional departmental divisions and the sharp distinction between officers and crew not only is likely to be required operationally, but can significantly enhance the social aspects of shipboard living.

Operating with smaller crews is likely to require greater crew continuity of employment. With proper use of team-building training, greater crew continuity should generally improve not only performance, but social and living conditions as well.

Drug and Alcohol Abuse

Careful management of alcohol availability and closer monitoring of the physical and emotional health of crew members will be essential for safety with smaller crews. One major potential advantage is that small crews imply greater mutual dependence for safe operation, so that peer pressure to be sober and fit for duty is likely to be greater, particularly if living areas are ergonomically designed to foster social interaction.

Adequacy of Coast Guard Human Factors Tools

Certification

The U.S. Coast Guard currently has no human factors models adequate for judging the implications of manning innovations for stress, fatigue, and boredom, or for assessing construction and manning plans with varying levels of shipboard technology. This study is one approach being pursued by the agency to provide a more appropriate basis for their decisions.

The challenge to the Coast Guard in carrying out its certificating responsibilities in a more highly automated environment will be substantial. Trends in shipboard automation should be thoroughly understood, and certification decisions should be based explicitly on new systems' training, use, and maintenance requirements. The functional analysis model described in Chapter 4 is a step in that direction. More research is required.

Accident Investigation

Current U.S. Coast Guard accident investigation tools may be insufficient to guide manning decisions related to stress, fatigue, and boredom. Recent research and development done for the Coast Guard has yielded promising approaches to accident investigation that take human factors into account (Dynamics Research Corporation, 1989). The Dynamics Research Corporation's Human Action Sequence Model allows accident investigators to specify the precise sequence of actions that resulted in an accident and to identify the many underlying causes. Human factors causes will be classified using some 68 different standardized categories.

This system is still under development. Once it is implemented, Coast Guard investigators will begin analyzing accidents and gathering detailed data relating accidents to human factors and adjusting ship design and operations to alleviate problems.

TRAINING AND CERTIFICATION OF SKILLS
FOR SHIPS OF THE FUTURE

The members of smaller crews must be more broadly skilled. First, small crews imply broader individual responsibilities. Second, vessels designed for smaller crews are generally technically more sophisticated. Training and certification of personnel qualifications must reflect these changes.

In most advanced shipping nations of Asia and northern Europe, both officers and unlicensed personnel are trained in the broad technical skills demanded by evolving technology and crewing practices. In the United States, by contrast, most formal training still reflects traditional departmental divisions of labor (enforced by law). However, officials of the U.S. Merchant Marine Academy and many in industry expect that a single class of broadly qualified watch officers (with training in both navigational and technical skills, as well as business and logistics) will be in charge of U.S.-flag ships of the future. Shipboard maintenance, now the province of highly trained licensed engineers, may become the responsibility of specialists (perhaps unlicensed technicians) and riding crews (Krinsky, 1989). Some shipping companies are already beginning to undertake their own training programs to broaden crew members' skills in response to new technology (American President Lines, 1989b).

New training, beyond that necessary to inculcate technical skill, will be needed. The U.S. Merchant Marine Academy has instituted courses in communication between masters and mates (White, 1989). The Maritime Institute of Technology and Graduate Studies (MITAGS) of the International Organization of Masters, Mates, and Pilots offers a course in shipboard management. American President Lines (1989b) has invested substantially in training crews of its new C-10 series vessels, with technical and management training as well as watch-keeping effectiveness. Many new automated shipboard systems have built-in capabilities for individual and team training, which permit operators to simulate training exercises and mentally rehearse typical and atypical conditions. These capabilities are similar to those found in U.S. Navy shipboard systems (Schuffel et al., 1989; Kristiansen et al., 1989; Grabowski, 1989).

The growing sophistication of crew members' responsibilities, many believe, will lead the Coast Guard to take more control over the precise qualifications of licensed and unlicensed personnel. Some qualifications may become more specialized to reflect differences in vessel type and service. For example, the Coast Guard might permit the introduction of additional skill requirements as employment conditions aboard ships requiring specialized knowledge. Periodic recertification of skills will become more important, to ensure that crew members develop and retain the necessary qualifications.

Training and Licensing Programs
of Advanced Shipping Nations

Fleets of the Federal Republic of Germany, Japan, and the Netherlands are among the most technically advanced in the world. Their training and licensing programs illustrate changes the United States should anticipate.

Japan

Japan has moved much further toward general purpose ratings and dual-qualified officers than any other nation. The initial experiments, in 1979, were succeeded by carefully planned steps toward a new "Hypothetical

Image of Seafarers." The newer Japanese vessels, with crews of 18, 16, or 14, are staffed largely with watch officers, dual-qualified officers who hold major qualifications in navigation or engineering but are operationally qualified to stand bridge or engine room watches. Even radio officers are being trained with watch-standing qualifications. All of them hold the license of watch officer, with the appropriate specialty (navigation, engineering, or radio).

Unlicensed personnel aboard these Japanese vessels are trained for general purpose work (Anonymous, 1989). Specially qualified unlicensed personnel are trained and certificated to head bridge watches in the open sea, although not in restricted waters. Companies themselves have borne most of the substantial cost of training for these new positions (Yamanaka and Gaffney, 1988).

The Federal Republic of Germany

The German shipping industry provides another illustration of training that may be required. In 1987, building on shipboard experiments conducted on vessels operated by Hapag-Lloyd AG, the industry shifted all programs for unlicensed personnel to general purpose training, eliminating separate deck and engine training. After three years, the neophyte sailor is qualified as a ship's mechanic. Further training, aboard ship and/or in a technical college can lead to an examination for the position of ship's foreman.

The Federal Republic of Germany has not moved completely to dual-qualified officers. The shipping industry there, however, expects highly automated state-of-the-art ships, with controls and monitors centralized on the bridge, to require ship management officers for the most efficient operation. This class of officer would be responsible for the entire ship—cargo, navigation, and maintenance—and would need both technical and navigational skills (Froese, 1989).

In 1986, as a first step in that direction, the industry, with government support, began offering officers with existing top-level deck and engine licenses training leading to medium-level credentials in the opposite specialties. The course involves eight months of practical training aboard ship, followed by one year of study at a technical university. (All officers are also required to complete the standard ship mechanics course.)

The Netherlands

In the Netherlands, all officers are now being trained in both deck and engine skills. The training is only partly integrated at present, but Dutch authorities expect to achieve full integration, with only one class of license for new officers, in the near future.

The four-year course for officers of large vessels includes a year at sea, with both technical and navigation experience. The traditional departmental distinctions are preserved to the extent that each graduate receives major and minor certifications (in navigation and technical qualifications), depending on the results of a series of final examinations. Further optional training is offered to bring graduates to fully integrated status. This training will soon be included in the standard four-year course, whose graduates will be certified as broadly qualified "maritime officers" or "ship managers" (Cross, 1988).

Some unlicensed crew members in the Netherlands are also trained in both deck and engine skills. For example, skilled ship mechanics, with general-purpose qualifications have been employed aboard Dutch ships since the late 1970s. Most vessels, however, carry only one or two ship mechanics to maintain mechanical systems. More recently, these personnel have been assigned as core crew aboard vessels manned largely with unskilled Third World crew members; in the guise of ship technicians, they may assume supervisory responsibilities.

Training in the United States

Training of seafarers in the United States is the responsibility of a wide variety of institutions. Federal- and state-supported academies and schools operated by labor unions train deck officers and engineers. Unlicensed personnel are trained mainly in union-run schools. The union schools are funded by the ship operating companies. Ship operators are increasingly becoming involved in training to meet the demands of high-technology ships.

Officer Training

Maritime academies and training schools. The maritime academies of the United States and the training schools operated by unions representing licensed personnel train the vast majority of their students in separate deck and engineering specialties. This pattern reflects the practices of the industry as enforced by manning laws and regulations. However, some steps have been taken to prepare officers for the future.

Since 1965, for example, the Merchant Marine Academy at Kings Point, New York, has offered students the opportunity to qualify for dual licenses in both deck and engine specialties. The intent of these intensive programs was to train officers highly skilled in both deck and engine specialties who could serve in either capacity. The proponents of this approach held that engineering competence would grow more—not less—vital as ships were automated and that the dual-licensed officer could provide that competence (personal communication, Walter McLean, U.S.

Merchant Marine Academy, February 1, 1990). This farsighted effort to ready the work force for the future, however, has been frustrated by Coast Guard licensing practices. While graduates of the program could qualify for both third mate and third engineer licenses, they were forced immediately to choose one path or the other to accumulate the service time required to become eligible for the next license level.

More fundamentally, the dual license in this form has been overtaken by evolving ship operations practices. The idea that modern vessels can safely traverse oceans without highly trained maintenance specialists aboard has gained acceptance worldwide. Many fleets have turned to shore-based personnel for major maintenance, leaving shipboard engineers in the more limited capacity of operating engineers. Thus, these programs have attracted fewer and fewer enrollees. The United States Merchant Marine Academy's dual license program was dropped for the class of 1993 but has been reinstated.

As a response to changing technology and management practices, the academy has instituted a pilot program to qualify ship operations officers for highly automated ships with control functions centralized on the bridge. Officers in the future, it is thought, will be in charge of entire ships—engines, navigation and communications, and management—rather than specializing in traditional departmental responsibilities. Notably, these officers will not need high-level training in engine operations. Rather, they will be trained to monitor engine functions, respond to alarms, and do elementary troubleshooting. The expectation is that the licensed engineer's role on these highly automated ships will become less important and that onboard maintenance may become the responsibility of an unlicensed engineering technician, with major maintenance the province of shore-based personnel (personal communication, Paul Krinsky, Superintendent, U.S. Merchant Marine Academy, November 15, 1989). This training course is expected to serve as the basis for a possible new category of license, that of watch officer (Krinsky, 1989).

Corporate training programs. Some companies have made their own increasing investments in training, reflecting the advance of world ship technology. For example, American President Lines (APL) in contracting with its unions to man its new, highly sophisticated C-9, J-9, and C-10 container ships negotiated high skill requirements. The company worked with established maritime schools to develop appropriate courses and required its C-10 officers to complete them. The investment in these courses was partially justified by the deck officers' union agreeing to give up rotation hiring in favor of long-term employment contracts (American President Lines, 1989a).

A notable feature of these agreements was the requirement that not only engineers but deck officers have training in diesel operations. To prepare for the acquisition of the C-9 vessels—APL's first diesels—engineers were sent to ride modern European ships for 30 days and received two weeks of factory training as well as special training in a variety of technical subjects, including exposure to a ship-handling simulator to gain knowledge of the vessels' maneuvering characteristics and navigation equipment (APL, 1989b).

With the J-9 container ships, the company developed a variety of team-building and "quality of work life" courses for officers. In addition, engineers spent 30 days each aboard the ships under their previous owners and received factory training on the engines and associated systems (Gaffney, 1989).

The C-10 vessels, up-to-date German "Ships of the Future," have a variety of unprecedented technical systems, including the largest diesel engines ever built and automated bridge equipment integrating the monitoring and control of all shipboard functions. Both deck officers and engineers received special training (American President Lines, 1989b). Experience with these new vessels, and the expectation of future operations with increasingly highly automated ships, led APL to establish the position of Director of Training, with a broad assignment to develop and carry out training policy. The company established a training library and contracted with MITAGS to develop and offer a series of courses stressing management skills, ship handling, and technical engineering competence (American President Lines, 1989c).

Much of the company's new training is centered around the operational demands of new integrated bridges, in which controls and monitors for all shipboard systems are centralized. For example, MITAGS is now developing "bridge organization and team management" courses for APL to be taught using simulators and other facilities of the U.S. Merchant Marine Academy and one or more of the union-run schools.

Training of Unlicensed Crew Members

Unlicensed personnel are trained mainly in schools operated by their unions. While the programs generally reflect traditional shipboard divisions of labor among deck, engine, and steward's departments, they have adapted to much new technology. For example, the Harry Lundeberg School of Seamanship, operated by the Seafarers International Union, recently introduced an electronics technician course to meet the maintenance requirements of automation and communication systems. It also offers courses in the use of computers for managing stewards' inventories, oil spill containment and cleanup, marine propulsion automation, and Sealift operations and maintenance (Seafarers Harry Lundeberg School of

Seamanship, 1990). Some of the union-run schools (including the Harry Lundeberg School) use ship-handling simulators in their unlicensed deck courses.

In the future, increasing flexibility of shipboard assignments may require unlicensed crew members to develop and use skills traditionally reserved to officers. For example, they may be members of tight-knit bridge operations teams with advanced skills in radar monitoring and open-sea watch-keeping.

Certifying Skills for the Ship of the Future

The Coast Guard's procedures in certifying crew members' skills will evolve to reflect the changing nature of shipboard work. Both officers' licenses and unlicensed documents will reflect the blurring of departmental distinctions and specify more precisely crew members' particular skills. To ensure that sophisticated skills remain up to date, the Coast Guard may demand more comprehensive recertification of skills on a periodic basis.

Most broadly, licenses and documents will certify the broad shipboard skills of the dual-qualified watch officer and the general purpose unlicensed crew member. With smaller crews and more highly integrated automated systems, the departmental distinction will fade.

At the same time, crew members will be called on to develop specialized skills to accommodate the sophisticated technology of modern ships. Licenses and documents will therefore carry endorsements certifying the attainment of special skills in ship handling, maintenance of electronic equipment, operation of specific engine types, and so on. Some companies and their unions have already negotiated agreements calling for successful completion of courses attesting to such additional skills as conditions of employment (American President Lines, 1990).

The advance of shipboard technology will tend to render skills obsolete as time passes, unless crew members receive new training or maintain their skills on the job. While officers are retested every five years to verify skills, unlicensed personnel's documents are good for life with no retesting. To ensure that sophisticated skills do not decay, the Coast Guard may be called upon in the future to recertify—through periodic testing—that skills remain fresh.

The existing training facilities have the capacity for much additional training; they are likely to play a strong role in maintaining and updating crew members' expertise.

AN EXAMPLE OF SUCCESSFUL TECHNOLOGY IMPLEMENTATION

The application of new technology to vessel operation has been a continuing process for hundreds, perhaps thousands, of years. Change has not always been accompanied by careful analysis of the associated safety impacts or human factors. However, the past 30 years does provide one significant example of technological change that has reduced work hours, lessened fatigue and boredom, and improved the quality of work life for seagoing personnel, while at the same time lowering manning requirements and operating expenses. This change involved the transition from essentially manually operated power plants to the fully automated, process-controlled power plants of today.

The steam-powered vessel of 30 years ago required an average of three, sometimes four, personnel on watch at any given time. The heat, noise, and vibration coupled with the four-on, eight-off watch rotation were not conducive to a healthy, stress-free environment. Watch duties were often boring, and the normal eight hours of watch were supplemented with overtime to complete maintenance tasks.

The transition from boiler water level controls (which replaced the watertender) to burner management systems (which replaced the fireman) to fully automated process control has led to the current unattended engine room operation. The switch from steam turbine propulsion to slow-speed diesel propulsion has assisted this transition

One U.S.-flag operator that recently completed the transition to fully automated power plants in its fleet reported overwhelming acceptance by its operating personnel. The average engine department aboard its vessels has been reduced from eight to five personnel. Previously, six of the eight engine department members aboard each ship were watch-standers. Their average work day was 11 1/2 hours. Now all five members of the engine department are day workers, and the work day averages 10 1/2 hours. Even more important, all members work together as a team, sharing the same work hours, meal times, and recreation times. Each enjoys a full and uninterrupted night's sleep every night. While the initial reaction to this change was one of apprehension, considerable effort was taken to train personnel in new assignments and to anticipate the human impacts of this change, which were as dramatic and as beneficial as the technological aspects.

FINDINGS

The introduction of new technology in ships should take account not only of the technology, but also of the human factors issues affected by the technology. Ships should be considered as sociotechnical systems, consisting of technologies, personnel, organizational structures, and an external environment. Change in any of these four subsystems should be accompanied by appropriate change in the others.

Relatively few human factors studies have been conducted in the maritime environment; most of those that have been conducted originated outside the United States. Data from aviation, other transportation industries, and other working environments may not accurately reflect human factors conditions and attendant performance aboard ships. Human factors research specific to the maritime industry is needed.

With appropriate training, organizational innovations, and ergonomic design, new vessel technology will not degrade safety. These approaches, for example, can reduce the potential problems of stress, fatigue, and boredom.

The U.S. Coast Guard, at present, does not have the necessary human factors analysis tools to make solid certification decisions about more highly automated ships.

Training programs will need to be altered as new technology is adopted, to reflect changes in work organization and the shipboard environment. For example, as departmental distinctions break down, officers and unlicensed personnel will need broader training, fitting them to meet the general needs of the ship, rather than narrowly specialized needs.

Licensing practices in the United States have sometimes inhibited innovation. As training programs shift their emphasis from specialization to broad competence, licensing will need to reflect this shift.

REFERENCES

Alliance of Independent Maritime Organizations. 1989. The invasion of the sixty hour work week standard and manning reductions in the U.S maritime industry. Statement Submitted to the Committee on the Effect of Smaller Crews on Maritime Safety, National Research Council, Washington, D.C. September 14.

American President Lines. 1989a. Labor contract. Report to the National Research Council Committee on the Effect of Smaller Crews on Maritime Safety, National Research Council, Washington, D.C. Mimeo. December 21.

American President Lines. 1989b. APL training. Report to the National Research Council Committee on the Effect of Smaller Crews on Maritime Safety, National Research Council, Washington, D.C. Mimeo. December 21.

American President Lines. 1989c. Marine Operations Department training program 1990. Mimeo. Oakland, California.

American President Lines. 1990. Memorandum from John G. Denham, Director Human Resources Development and Training (Subject: Trip report 3 March through 9 March 1990). Mimeo. March 26.

Anonymous. 1989. The modernization of the seafarer's system in Japan. Paper presented at Maritime Training Forum Europe '89, Amsterdam. June 20.

Beetham, E. H. 1989. Bridge manning. Seaways. February.

Bobb, John. 1989. Statement of the International Organization of Masters, Mates, and Pilots on manning before the Marine Board of the National Research Council, National Research Council, Washington, D.C. September 14.

Colquhoun, W. P., J. Rutenfranz, H. Goethe, B. Neidhart, R. Condon, R. Plett, and P. Knauth. 1988. Work at sea: A study of sleep, and of circadian rhythms in physiological and psychological functions, in watch keepers on merchant vessels (I. Watchkeeping on board ships: A methodological approach). International Archives of Occupational and Environmental Health 60:321-329.

Condon, R., W. P. Colquhoun, R. Plett, D. DeVol, and N. Fletcher. 1988. Work at sea: A study of sleep, and of circadian rhythms in physiological and psychological functions, in watch keepers on merchant vessels (IV. Rhythms in performance and alertness). International Archives of Occupational and Environmental Health 60:405-411.

Connaughton, Sean T. 1988. Federal rules on operating a commercial vessel while intoxicated. Proceedings of the Marine Safety Council 45(2), February/March.

Cross, S. J. 1988 Nautical training in the Netherlands: Present and future. Seaways

DeGreene, Kenyon B. 1973. Sociotechnical Systems. Factors in Analysis, Design, and Management. Englewood Cliffs, New Jersey: Prentice-Hall.

Dynamics Research Corporation. The role of human factors in marine casualties. Unpublished U.S. Coast Guard R&D Report, Contract No. N00024-85-D-4373. 5 June 1989.

Fletcher, N., W. P. Colquhoun, P. Knauth, D. DeVol, and R. Plett. 1988. Work at sea: A study of sleep, and of circadian rhythms in physiological and psychological functions, in watch keepers on merchant vessels (VI. A sea trial of an alternative watchkeeping system for the merchant marine). International Archives of Occupational and Environmental Health 61:51-57.

Folsom, D. L. 1988. Vessel automation control reliability, reduced manning, maintenance, and operator responsibility. Memorandum from Commander, First Coast Guard District, to Commandant, U.S. Coast Guard. December 19.

Froese, Jens. Training for advanced ships. Paper presented at Maritime Training Forum Europe '89, Amsterdam, June 20.

Gaffney, Michael E. 1989. Effective manning at American President Lines. Report from American President Lines to U.S. Department of Transportation, Maritime Administration, Office of Technology Assessment. Cooperative Agreement No. MA-11727, Report No. MA-RD-840-89008. June 6.

Grabowski, Martha. 1989. Decision aiding technology and integrated bridge design. Proceedings of the Society of Naval Architects and Marine Engineers Spring Meeting/STAR Symposium. New Orleans, Louisiana. April 12-15.

Grove, T. W. 1989. U.S. flag ship of the future: Concepts, features and issues. Paper presented at 1989 Spring Meeting and STAR Symposium, Society of Naval Architects and Marine Engineers, New Orleans, Louisiana, April 12-15.

Hillman, John L. 1989. Letter from President, Exxon Seaman's Union, to Charles Bookman, Executive Director, Marine Board, National Research Council, Washington, D.C. September 21.

Hockey, Glyn Robert John. 1986. Changes in operator efficiency as a function of environmental stress, fatigue, and circadian rhythms. Handbook of Perception and Human Performance. New York: John Wiley & Sons. pp. 44-1ff.

International Transportation Workers' Federation. 1990. Submission to the Eighth Session of the ILO/IMO Joint Committee on Training (JCT8), Geneva, 17-21, September.

Krinsky, Paul L. 1989. Letter to Eugene McCormick, President, Lykes Brothers Steamship Company. December 11.

Kristiansen, Svein, Egil Rensvik, and Lars Mathisen. 1989. Integrated total control of the bridge. Paper presented at Annual Meeting of the Society of Naval Architects and Marine Engineers, New York, November 15-18.

Low, A., W. H. G. Goethe, J. Rutenfranz, and W. P. Colquhoun. 1987. Human factors: Effects of watch keeping—results of studies for the German Ship of the Future. Paper presented at Society of Naval Architects and Marine Engineers Ship Operations Management and Economics Symposium, September 1987.

National Transportation Safety Board (NTSB). 1989. Safety study: Passenger vessels operating from U.S. ports. Report no. NTSB/SS-89/01. Washington, D.C.: NTSB.

Nautical Institute. 1989a. Bridge manning: Recommendations by Council, December 1988. Seaways, February.

Nautical Institute. 1989b. The Nautical Institute on improving standards of bridge operation: Recommendations by Council, December 1988. Seaways, February.

Parasuraman, Raja. 1986. Vigilance, monitoring, and search. In Handbook of Perception and Human Performance. New York: John Wiley & Sons. pp. 43-1ff.

Parasuraman, Raja. 1987. Human-computer monitoring. Human Factors 29(6):695-706.

Perkins, M. R. 1988. Vessel automation control reliability, reduced manning, maintenance, and operator responsibility: First endorsement on MSO Portland's ltr 16711 of 6 Dec 88. Memorandum from Commanding Officer, Marine Safety Office, Portland, Maine, to Commandant, U.S. Coast Guard.

Pettin, Thomas J. 1987. Fatigue as the cause of marine accidents, 1981-1985. U.S. Coast Guard, Marine Investigation Division. March.

Rutenfranz, J., R. Plett, P. Knauth, R. Condon, D. DeVol, N. Fletcher, S. Eickhoff, K.-H. Schmidt, R. Donis, and W. P. Colquhoun. 1988. Work at sea: A study of sleep, and of circadian rhythms in physiological and psychological functions, in watch keepers on merchant vessels (II. Sleep duration, and subjective ratings of sleep quality). International Archives of Occupational and Environmental Health 60:331-339.

Salvendy, G., ed. 1987. Handbook of Human Factors. New York: Wiley Interscience.

Sanders, M. S., and E. J. McCormick. 1986. Human Factors in Engineering and Design. New York: McGraw Hill.

Schuffel, H., J. P. A. Boer, and L. van Breda. 1989. The ship's wheelhouse of the nineties: The navigation performance and mental workload of the officer of the watch. Journal of the Institute of Navigation 42:1(60-72).

Seafarers Harry Lundeberg School of Seamanship. 1990. Catalog 1990. Piney Point, Maryland.

Thackray, R. I. 1981. The stress of boredom and monotony: A consideration of the evidence. Psychosomatic Medicine 43:165-176.

U.S. Coast Guard. 1988. Programs for chemical drug and alcohol testing of commercial vessel personnel. Federal Register 53(131).

U.S. Department of Transportation. 1989. Transportation-related sleep research. Report to the Senate Committee on Appropriations and the House Committee on Appropriations. March.

Vail, Bruce. 1988. Crew cuts please ship lines but take toll on seafarers. Journal of Commerce. November 28.

White, David F. 1989. Ship course stresses teamwork on bridge. Journal of Commerce. August 29.

Yamanaka, Keiko, and Michael Gaffney. 1988. Effective manning in the Orient. Report from American President Lines to U.S. Department of Transportation, Maritime Administration, Office of Technology Assessment. Cooperative Agreement No. MA-11727, Report No. MA-RD-770-87052. March 15.

4

Establishing Safe Crew Levels

The U.S. Coast Guard relies on a combination of laws, regulations, tradition, and informal policy guidance to set crew levels. This piecemeal approach was effective in the past when technological change was slow and manning scales generous. However, it is not a sound basis for decisions that must accommodate changing technology and minimal manning.

Systems engineering techniques are beginning to be used in manning decisions by shipping companies. These techniques include the construction of computer models of vessel operations, so that shipboard functions and tasks can be precisely specified and evaluated for a ship of a given design, trade, and level of technology under normal and emergency conditions. Manning scales can be established accordingly.

This chapter reviews current regulatory procedures for Coast Guard manning determinations and discusses the advantages of systems engineering as an alternative. It also presents a functional task analysis model developed and tested by the committee. With appropriate extension and refinement, such a model could offer regulators, owners, and operators the tools for making manning decisions on a sound analytical basis. As ship operating technology and crewing grow more complex, such an approach will become increasingly necessary.

U.S. COAST GUARD CERTIFICATION PROCEDURES

The U.S. government controls vessel manning through statutes, which are implemented in regulations and interpreted by judicial rulings. The regulations are promulgated and enforced by the U.S. Coast Guard. In addition, the Coast Guard specifies the minimum complement of licensed and unlicensed persons necessary for safe operation of each vessel; these requirements are set out by each vessel's Certificate of Inspection (COI), as required by the International Convention on the Safety of Life at Sea (SOLAS).

Until the late 1970s, most U.S.-flag vessels sailed with crew complements well above the levels specified in Coast Guard-issued COIs as necessary for safe navigation. Recent attempts to cut costs have brought dramatic crew reductions, however, with some ships operating at or near their COI minimum.

The Coast Guard anticipates that future technical and organizational innovations will result in ships with crews of a dozen or fewer highly trained specialists to operate the vessel and conduct emergency maintenance, and that routine maintenance and cargo operations will be the responsibilities of shore-based personnel (Connaughton, 1987). Current statutes and regulatory procedures will be inadequate to accommodate these innovations (see Chapter 5).

Regulatory Procedures

The owner or operator of any ship that requires a COI must submit an application for inspection to a Coast Guard Officer-in-Charge, Marine Inspection (OCMI). The owner also must submit descriptions of the vessel and the kind of trade in which it will be used. On the basis of these descriptions, the vessel is placed in a particular class or inspection category (e.g., freight vessel, tank vessel, or offshore supply vessel). Depending on its class and intended service, the vessel's design and construction plans are reviewed by either the Coast Guard's Marine Safety Center or the American Bureau of Shipping, acting on behalf of the Coast Guard.

Once the vessel's class is determined, the owner or operator can develop a manning plan according to standards set out in the Coast Guard *Marine Safety Manual*. The plan is submitted to the OCMI in the region where the vessel is being built. The OCMI then sets a conditional manning level, which is subject to revision if an OCMI later decides a change is necessary for safety reasons.

The OCMI, in establishing manning levels, considers applicable statutes (especially Part G, Title 46, of the U.S. Code [U.S.C.]), regulations (46 CFR Part 15), and Coast Guard policies set out in the *Marine Safety Manual* and Navigation and Inspection Circulars (NVICs). Special conditions such as shipboard automation and monitoring equipment, route and trade characteristics, maintenance and support facilities, and self-imposed operating limitations can also be considered, along with the documented history of any vessel being modified or reflagged.

Ordinarily, the OCMI's manning determination is a routine matter. However, if the manning request involves innovation (the first ship of a series, reduced manning on an existing ship, or a ship whose class is not covered in policy guidelines) the OCMI forwards the request to the Merchant Vessel Personnel Division at Coast Guard Headquarters.

When the OCMI and headquarters reviews are complete and the vessel has completed sea trials, its manning complement is placed on the COI. The complement specified on the COI represents the minimum number of personnel considered necessary for safe operation, along with the license and document grades and endorsements those personnel must hold. (The COI will also specify the maximum numbers of "other persons in the crew" and "persons in addition to the crew," according to the available accommodations and lifeboat capacity.)

The Coast Guard normally does not specify manning levels outside the deck and engineering departments (such as stewards), except for radio officers, which are required by law and international agreement aboard most ocean-going commercial vessels.

In 1983, a significant change in the manning statutes was made, partly to accommodate increased number of requests for reduced manning. Previously, the law required manning levels to be determined as the minimum necessary for safe *navigation*. In that year, a recodification of 46 U.S.C. resulted in a requirement to set manning levels as the minimum "necessary for safe *operation*" (46 U.S.C. § 8101(a); emphasis added). As a result of this change, the agency pays more attention to maintenance plans in manning determinations today than it did in the past. (Well maintained equipment is especially vital with smaller crews.) In most cases, the agency requires a strong preventive maintenance program.

Owners or operators wishing to reduce manning on existing ships through automation must submit an application, together with required documentation showing how the vessel may be operated safely at the reduced level. Often the Coast Guard grants conceptual approval of such plans before investments in vessel modifications are made. After the modifications are made, the systems must undergo a trial period to prove their reliability and safety. During this period, which may last for 6 months or more, the owner must keep detailed records of the vessel's operating history, crew overtime, equipment casualties, and other information. A Coast Guard inspector sails aboard the vessel, observing routine operations and emergency drills to assess the adequacy of the reduced manning.

Manning Reductions to Date

Deck Department

Deck department reductions to date have been the simplest crew reductions to evaluate and have generally been processed in the field by the cognizant OCMIs. The most common reduction at present involves the addition of devices such as constant-tension winches, a watch call system, and sanitary and coffee facilities on the bridge. If these additions are approved, up to three ordinary seamen (OSs) may be removed from the vessel's COI. If they are removed, the COI may be further amended to allow two of the required six able-bodied seamen (ABs) to be "specially trained" OSs (with the physical and training qualifications of able seamen, but holding ordinary seaman endorsements). Some day-working maintenance workers may be required in lieu of the removed ordinary seamen.

Engine Department

Engine department reductions are more complex and are usually referred to Coast Guard Headquarters for approval. Technical standards are set out in 46 CFR Part 62 (Vital System Automation, § 62.50–Manning). Such reductions are of three types: (1) elimination of the requirement for fire/watertenders on steam-powered vessels; (2) minimally attended engine room operation (with the addition of a central engine room monitoring and control station) to eliminate the need for several or all unlicensed watch standing personnel; and (3) periodically unattended engine room operation, with a variety of labor saving devices and monitoring and control systems so that the engine room can be left unattended for prolonged periods.

Maintenance Departments

Use of a maintenance department (see Chapter 1) increases operational flexibility and permits reduced manning through reassignment of personnel. Maintenance departments are subject to the approval of Coast Guard Headquarters.

Future Manning Reductions

In the relatively near future, more complex manning reductions are likely to be requested. For example, the Coast Guard may receive requests to implement the dual-qualified, watch officer concept on the Japanese model. In the long run, the advance of technology will generally tend to erode the departmental distinctions aboard ships.

A FUNCTIONAL MODEL FOR ASSESSING CREW LEVELS

The committee developed a functional model for task analysis and evaluated it by applying it to data from two actual ships. The model proved easy to use, comprehensive, and accurate. With further development, it could be used by the U.S. Coast Guard and by ship owners and operators to determine, systematically and reliably, the minimum manning levels for a variety of ship types and operating conditions. Additional work, for example, would make it more robust and flexible and would add risk or hazard analysis information.

The thorough assessment of shipboard functions and tasks permitted by the model would be particularly useful to the Coast Guard in setting manning levels. An initial determination of crew requirements could be made using the model with data from expert opinions, and then confirmed during sea trials by entering actual voyage data into the model.

Certification for smaller crews, using the model, could be based on actual performance, rather than on judgment alone. Such a process might have two steps. First, the owner or operator would submit for Coast Guard conditional approval a functional analysis of crew activities (with specified crew numbers and structure, skills and training, voyage profile, and operation and maintenance plans). Upon conditional approval, the vessel would be subjected to sea trials of up to six months, with logs of crew activities. The data from the trials would be used to validate the results obtained from the model.

Such a procedure would give the Coast Guard a sound basis for decisions, explicitly taking account of the vessel's type, voyage profile, level of technology, and operating conditions. It would replace the current system of reliance on a patchwork of manning statutes, informal policy, and tradition. It would thus permit the U.S. shipping industry to take advantage of new technology without sacrificing the safety of vessels or shipboard personnel.

Shipboard Task Analysis

Over the last decade, the maritime community has combined concerns about the safety of navigation in an increasingly complex environment with concerns about more efficient operations. One trend toward reducing operational costs and increasing operational safety focuses on applying systems engineering.

Systems engineering normally begins with a *requirements analysis* to determine the mission and functional requirements of present and future systems to help identify the tasks that must be supported (Figure 4-1). Next, a *task analysis* identifies the tasks presently performed and those

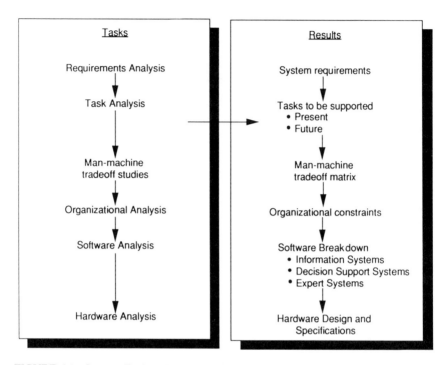

FIGURE 4-1   Systems Engineering Approaches to Shipboard Manning.

to be performed in the future. During the task analysis, a *man-machine tradeoff study* is performed to determine which tasks will be performed by people and which by machines.

The next step is an *organizational analysis* to determine how the human and machine tasks of the future will be supported in the organization. A *software analysis* then focuses on the information processing requirements of the tasks allocated to machines to determine, for example, which of the machine tasks can be supported with conventional software, and which are more amenable to decision support systems or expert systems implementation. Finally, a *hardware analysis* is performed to identify the appropriate hardware.

The Committee's Functional Model

The committee's model is a task analysis tool applicable to all ship types, classes, and trades. It permits the assessment of manning over an entire voyage and in emergencies such as shipboard fires. Appendix E describes earlier shipboard task analyses.

The model uses a taxonomy of 10 general functions, broken down into subfunctions, and sub-subfunctions that describe all aspects of shipboard operations across a broad spectrum of cargo, ship, and voyage types (Table 4-1). The general skills and time required to perform these functions are then determined to yield qualitative and quantitative minimum manning requirements.

The model was applied to two actual ships. First, the taxonomy of functions was used to code two sets of data from American President Lines (APL): 30 months of actual maintenance data and summary deck operations data developed by a panel of APL ship's officers (described later in this chapter). Later, the taxonomy was used to code engineering and deck operations data developed by a panel of Exxon ship's officers for a specific Exxon ship and voyage profile (also described below). This coding demonstrated the comprehensiveness of the initial taxonomy and resulted in some refinements.

Description of the Model

Ten major shipboard functions identified in Table 4-1 are: cargo, ballast, navigation, main engine operations, auxiliary equipment operations, long-range radio operations, deck operations, general operations, general administration, and hotel functions. Data were collected from APL and Exxon for each function, subfunction, and sub-subfunction, and for each of three voyage phases—at dock, transiting restricted waters, and at sea. The time it took to perform any specific function was recorded for the range (i.e, the minimum and maximum times) and for the average time required. The maximum number of people required to perform the function at any specific time was recorded, along with the number of persons of any given skill level required. For example, if the average time for a given function (such as loading cargo) was four hours, and one person of a given skill classification (a licensed deck officer, for example) worked on the function full-time, while another of the same skill classification was required for two hours, 1.5 would be entered as the number of people of that skill classification required to perform that function. Five general skill classifications were used: licensed (N1) and unlicensed (N2) deck personnel; licensed (E1) and unlicensed (E2) engineering personnel; and steward's department personnel (G).

Any tasks that must be done in conjunction with the specific task were also noted. Where the manning requirements for a specific function under restricted visibility were greater than those in good visibility (for example, while transiting restricted waters), the restricted visibility requirements were recorded. Above the function coding portion of the form, spaces were provided for indicating whether tasks were mandatory or discretionary for

TABLE 4-1 Shipboard Functions Identified in Committee's Functional Model

TASKS TO BE EVALUATED

1.0 CARGO
    1.1 On-load
    1.2 Off-load
    1.3 Maintenance of cargo equipment/deck stores/wares and ballast tank cleaning and repairs of cargo, desk equipment, stores and wares
    1.4 Record keeping (port logs)
    1.5 Repair
        1.5.1 Reefer-maintenance
        1.5.2 Inspection

2.0 BALLAST
    2.1 On-load
    2.2 Off-load

3.0 NAVIGATION
    3.1 Track keeping
        3.1.1 Day—good visibility
        3.1.2 Night—good visibility
        3.1.3 Restricted visibility
    3.2 Maneuvering
        3.2.1 Chart correction
    3.3 Collision avoidance
    3.4 Voyage/passage planning
    3.5 Record/chart keeping and update/bridge logs/charts and navigation information
    3.6 Maintenance
        3.6.1 PMS
        3.6.2 Unscheduled
    3.7 Test vital systems
        3.7.1 Prior to leaving port
        3.7.2 Prior to entering port
    3.8 Bridge housekeeping
    3.9 Weather monitoring
        3.9.1 Reporting
        3.9.2 Planning
    3.10 Hull Performance
        3.10.1 Monitoring
        3.10.2 Maneuvering
        3.10.3 Planning
    3.11 Training (equipment operations, procedure review, standard operations)

4.0 ENGINE OPERATIONS
    4.1 Operations—routine and watch standing
    4.2 Maintenance
        4.2.1 Unscheduled
        4.2.2 PMS
    4.3 Record keeping
        4.3.1 Records and record keeping
        4.3.2 Soundings

5.0 AUXILIARY EQUIPMENT OPERATIONS (all non-main engine propulsion equipment)
    5.1 Generators
        5.1.1 Operations
        5.1.2 Unscheduled maintenance
        5.1.3 PMS
    5.2 Fuel oil systems
        5.2.1 Operations
        5.2.2 Unscheduled maintenance
        5.2.3 PMS
    5.3 Boilers
        5.3.1 Operations
        5.3.2 Unscheduled maintenance
        5.2.3 PMS
    5.4 Evaporators
        5.4.1 Operations
        5.4.2 Unscheduled maintenance
        5.4.3 PMS
    5.5 Refrigerator/air conditioning
        5.5.1 Operations
        5.5.2 Unscheduled maintenance
        5.5.3 PMS
    5.6 Sewage systems
        5.6.1 Operations
        5.6.2 Unscheduled maintenance
        5.6.3 PMS
    5.7 Inert gas systems
        5.7.1 Operations
        5.7.2 Unscheduled maintenance
        5.7.3 PMS
    5.8 Electrical/electrical control systems
        5.8.1 Operations
        5.8.2 Unscheduled maintenance
        5.8.3 PMS

TABLE 4-1, Continued

5.9 Tools and test equipment
    5.9.1 Operations
    5.9.2 Unscheduled maintenance
    5.9.3 PMS
5.10 Pumps
    5.10.1 Operations
    5.10.2 Unscheduled maintenance
    5.10.3 PMS
5.11 Fuel transfer
5.12 Record keeping

6.0 LONG RANGE RADIO OPERATIONS

7.0 DECK OPERATIONS
  7.1 Docking/undocking
  7.2 Mooring/unmooring (offshore)
  7.3 Anchoring/heaving-in
  7.4 Helicopter operations
  7.5 Underwater lighting
  7.6 Tugs/crane using
  7.7 Preparation for going into yard/drydock

8.0 GENERAL OPERATIONS
  8.1 Drills (lifeboat, firefighting, etc.)
  8.2 Maintenance (lifeboats)
  8.3 Safety tours
  8.4 Vessel fabric maintenance (paint, chip. grease, coat)
  8.5 Deck equipment maintenance (lights, structure, mooring equipment, anchor, bow transfer, gangway, capstans, windlass)
  8.6 Line and wire maintenance
  8.7 Stores and supplies
    8.7.1 Handling

    8.7.2 Storage
    8.7.3 Ordering
  8.8 Other training
  8.9 Medical
  8.10 Bunkering
  8.11 Safety equipment maintenance, gas test meters, and gauging equipment
  8.12 Vessel structure maintenance/repair
  8.13 Steering gear maintenance
  8.14 Cleaning/wash down
    8.14.1 Deck
    8.14.2 Engine room housekeeping
  8.15 Supervise shore personnel/gangs
  8.16 Stability and cargo planning

9.0 GENERAL ADMINISTRATION
  9.1 Financial
  9.2 Labor relations
  9.3 Meetings
    9.3.1 Shipboard management
    9.3.2 Safety
  9.4 Payroll
  9.5 Regulatory requirement monitoring/inspections/ walkarounds with inspection regulatory authorities
  9.6 Special projects

10.0 HOTEL FUNCTIONS
  10.1 Catering
  10.2 Accommodation and space clearing
  10.3 Management
  10.4 Provisioning
  10.5 Maintenance

the given time periods, and whether they were intended to be performed by the ship's crew or by a riding crew.

To determine the manning requirements, the ship voyage profile and operating conditions were first specified. For each shipboard function, the average time required was recorded, then multiplied by its frequency of occurrence per voyage. This data was then multiplied by the number of persons of a given skill classification needed to perform the function. This gave the total amount of time required by persons of a given skill classification to perform that specific function during the voyage. Dividing this figure by the total number of voyage days yielded the average time per day required for that function; dividing this number by the average number of true working hours per day per person in that skill classification gave the number of persons required per day. In the validation studies, described below under the heading "Evaluation of the Model," a 10-hour working day was used as a baseline, reflecting experience at the two companies.

This procedure was repeated for each function and skill classification. For each skill classification, the total number of persons per day required across all functions yielded the total number of persons of that skill required to operate the vessel safely and to support the requisite shipboard work load. Summing these totals across all five skill classifications (N1, N2, E1, E2, and G) yielded the total manning requirement for that ship, that voyage profile, and that set of given operating conditions.

Based on the two validation studies described below, it appears that simply adding the data across all phases provides an accurate estimate of the minimum manning requirements for a particular ship. The data can also be calculated for different phases of the voyage (at dock, transiting restricted waters, at sea) to determine if different voyage phases require different manning levels. Similarly, if some functions are routinely performed by a riding crew, separate calculations can be performed to determine the appropriate manning tradeoffs between the ship's crew and the riding crew.

Emergency Conditions

The procedures described apply to normal operating conditions only. New state-of-the-art ships may be able to operate under normal operating conditions with crews that are too small to handle emergency conditions. Based on expert opinions of the persons who participated in the development and two initial validation studies of the model, the ability to fight shipboard fires will require larger crews than normal operations on some highly automated ships. As a result, manning requirements for emergency conditions—particularly fighting shipboard fires—were analyzed. This analysis required estimating both the manning requirements for operating the ship while the fire is being fought and those for actually fighting the fire. Two types of fire (an engine room fire from a broken high-pressure fuel line and a container fire on deck) were analyzed.

Operating Conditions Affecting Manning

In developing and validating the model, the committee identified a number of operating conditions bearing on manning:

- *Operating procedures*—i.e., will certain maintenance functions be performed by the ship's crew, a riding crew, or a shore gang when the ship is in port?
- *Maintenance concept employed*—i.e., is a maintenance department in use?

- *Crew/role flexibility*—i.e., to what extent can persons perform both deck and engineering functions, or possess dual certification?
- *Crew continuity*—i.e., to what extent do crew members stay together, or train as a crew?
- *Ship familiarity*—i.e., to what extent do crew members sail on the same ship or same class of ship?
- *Regulatory and union contract requirements and restrictions*—i.e., interdepartmental flexibility, employment continuity aboard the same ship or class of ship, familiarity with the specific ship.
- *Personnel selection procedures/criteria*—i.e., skills, physical condition, personality factors, expectation levels.
- *Job design*—e.g., chief mate's responsibilities.
- *Training/proficiency*—i.e., to what extent do crew members receive training/education to upgrade skills, or cross-train to broaden their skills?

Evaluation of the Model

To test the model's utility, it was used to determine manning requirements for two different ships, operated by different companies, with different voyage profiles. Both shipping organizations had already undertaken extensive manning studies and both had high confidence in their manning requirements. The first ship used was an American President Lines C-9 container ship operating between the west coast of the United States and the Far East. The second ship was an Exxon product tanker on a 14-day coastwise run between Houston, Texas, and a variety of southeastern U.S. ports.

The committee's first objective was to determine whether the functional model was adequate to accommodate all functions performed on both ships during routine voyages. As noted above, the model was found to be comprehensive and required only minor refinement, mainly the addition of some sub-subfunctions (primarily in Function 5, Auxiliary Equipment Operations).

The second objective was to determine whether the model would produce results that accurately reflected manning requirements. This determination was made somewhat differently for the two ships, as described below.

American President Lines C-9 Container Ship Study

American President Lines (APL) had conducted an extensive study of one of its C-9 container ships by carefully collecting actual maintenance data over a 30-month period, during 25 voyages. In addition, a panel of C-9 ship's officers had classified and developed consensus expert opinions on the functions and manning requirements for all bridge operations. With assistance from APL personnel who had worked on the computerization and coding of the C-9 data, the data were recoded using the committee's functional model codes. These data were compiled and used to determine manning requirements for the subject C-9 ship. These calculated requirements matched its actual manning scale, both in number (21 people) and crew organization. They also suggested that under different operating conditions (i.e., those that would provide crew continuity or familiarity with the C-9), manning requirements could be reduced.

Four major types of fires were identified to be of concern: (1) high-pressure fuel line break in the engine room, (2) generator fire, (3) stores fire, and (4) container fires (from internal combustion or stack exhaust sparks). Of these, the engine room fire from a high-pressure fuel line break was judged to be the most labor-intensive. To operate the ship while fighting the fire, two persons—the master and a helmsman—would be required for machinery operations. To fight the fire, an emergency coordinator and two three-man hose teams, each with a squad leader, would be required. This estimate results in a total of 11 people, well below present manning.

Exxon Mixed Product Tanker Study

Through careful observation and study of many of their voyages, the officers of an Exxon mixed product tanker had developed expert opinions about the time and skill requirements for the various ship operating functions. Several of the ship's officers and several senior ship captains from other Exxon tankers helped the committee complete the function analysis forms for the model. The data thus gathered were used to determine the vessel's minimum manning requirements.

The vessel's present manning is 18 people: 4 N1 (1 master, 3 mates), 6 N2 (6 ABs), 4 E1 (1 chief engineer, 3 assistant engineers), 2 E2 (1 engine unlicensed, 1 pumpman), and 2 G (2 stewards).[1] The Exxon group believed that two of the ABs were not actually needed, and that with some policy modification it would be possible to operate with only one steward. The vessel's COI authorizes a crew of 14, based on the use of a maintenance department and only 1 steward (the maintenance department having eliminated the need for one AB).

The manning requirements determined by the model are 4 N1, 3 N2, 4.5 E1, 2 E2, and 1.5 G, for a total crew of 15. Rounding up to the nearest whole person in each skill classification brings the total number to 16. In summary, the model supported the Exxon team's belief that the number of N2s (ABs) could be reduced by at least two. By requiring the crew to do

---

[1] Shipboard positions were classed as N1 (licensed deck), N2 (unlicensed deck), E1 (licensed engine), E2 (unlicensed engine), and G (stewards).

more of their own housekeeping, the number of stewards could be reduced to 1, for a total of 15.

After reviewing the model's output, the Exxon team agreed that, with minor changes in task distribution, the ideal minimum crew would be a crew of 15: 4 N1 (1 master, 3 mates), 4 N2 (4 ABs), 4 E1 (chief engineer, 3 assistant engineers), and 2 E2 (1 engine unlicensed, 1 pumpman).

By changing maintenance procedures and assigning painting and chipping to shore-based personnel, manning could be reduced by an additional N2 (1 AB), for a total of 14.

The vessel's manning requirements for an engine room fire resulting from a high-pressure fuel line break were analyzed and found to be the same as the those of the APL C-9, or a total of 11 people, which is below the minimum manning level of 14 for normal operations.

The tanker study not only validated the model's utility in determining minimum manning requirements, it also demonstrated how the model could be used as a management tool to make manning adjustments for greater operating efficiency.

It should be remembered that the data used in the tanker validation study were based mainly on expert opinion, backed up by some recorded data and considerable deliberate observation by the team of experts and their colleagues aboard the vessel. A next logical step would be to conduct a validation study of the model, based on systematically recorded voyage data for the same vessel.

The Model's Utility

The validation studies show that the model provides an accurate estimate of minimum manning levels. Manning by phase (at dock, transiting restricted waters, or at sea) can be calculated, and tradeoffs (e.g., ship crew tasks versus riding crew tasks) can be analyzed.

Once the data for a given voyage profile and set of operating conditions have been collected and analyzed, the model can be used to estimate the effect of new technology (i.e., unattended engine room, decision support systems), alternative voyage profiles, or revised operating conditions. The model can thus be used as a management tool to assess the impact of changes (or proposed changes) on safe manning requirements.

The model also would allow the U.S. Coast Guard, ship owners, and operators to identify manning-sensitive tasks, manning-rich areas (candidates for manning reductions), simultaneous tasks (time-substitutable tasks), tasks performed by similarly skilled personnel (skill-substitutable tasks), and tasks requiring similar time to perform (duration-substitutable tasks). Such tradeoff studies could assess the manning impact of new technology; of new ship designs, layouts, facilities configurations; or new shipboard procedures, processes, and controls. Safety concerns could be highlighted, or safety issues addressed, by maintaining minimum hourly performance requirements in the data.

Limitations of the Model

The work to date supports the notion that the functional model developed can be used by the U.S. Coast Guard, ship owners, and operators in determining minimum manning levels for a variety of ship types. However, there are a number of limitations to the model as it exists:

• The model has been validated with two sets of shipping data: one from a product tanker in the domestic trade, one from a container ship trading between the U.S. West Coast and the Far East. Before the model is accepted for general use, it needs to be validated against actual voyage data for a wider variety of ship types, trades, designs, and under varying operating conditions.

• A more thorough empirical analysis of emergency and restricted visibility conditions needs to be conducted with the model; only anecdotal emergency and restricted visibility information were used during the initial validation studies.

• The model is not at present tied to risk or hazards analysis data (or a risk or hazards analysis model). If it were, model-recommended manning estimates could be compared with preferred manning structures (from a risk or hazards analysis perspective) to produce qualitative comparisons and rankings between alternative manning structures.

• There is no formal mechanism within the model for ranking and comparing alternative manning structures. This decision support capability could be incorporated into the model, so that ranked recommended manning alternatives, with explanations, would be the model's output.

• At present, the model does not accommodate uncertain or incomplete information. Neither does it accommodate decision making under time pressure. Both capabilities could be incorporated.

• The model does not offer a graphical representation of shipboard tasks over time, which would be helpful in visualizing those performed at different times, at the same time, or by similarly skilled personnel. In addition, beneath the graphic representation, a link between the model and cost-benefit analysis data would be helpful, so that recommendations for time- and personnel-substitutable tasks could be linked to cost data for a quantitative and qualitative comparison.

These limitations do not suggest that the model as it presently exists is not a useful preliminary tool in arriving at minimum manning estimates. However, additional validation studies need to be conducted before it is adopted for general use. The added enhancements may improve its robustness, decision support capabilities, and ease of use.

FINDINGS

In establishing safe crew levels, the government and industry need to consider demands on the crew: each vessel's technology, type of service, crew skills, and quality of management and management programs. Systems engineering methods, including functional task analysis, offer an objective basis for such determinations. The model developed is one approach to implementing systems engineering approaches to determining safe ship manning levels.

REFERENCES

Connaughton, Sean. 1987. Coast guard merchant vessel manning. Paper presented at 1987 Ship Operations, Management and Economics International Symposium, U.S. Merchant Marine Academy, Kings Point, New York. September 17-18.

Denny, M. 1987. Shipboard productivity methods. U.S. Department of Transportation, Maritime Administration, Washington, D.C. Volumes 1-3. February.

Liverpool Polytechnic and Collaborating Colleges. 1986. Technology and Manning for Safe Ship Operations, Volumes 1 and 2. Department of Transport. London. November.

Schuffel, H., J. P. A. Boer, and L. van Breda, 1989. The ship's wheelhouse of the nineties: The navigation performance and mental workload of the officer of the watch. Journal of Navigation 42(1):60-72.

Williams, V. E. 1983. Crew Rationalization Study: ODS Liner Vessels. U.S. Department of Transportation, Maritime Administration, Office of Research and Development, Washington, D.C. April

Yamanaka, K., and M. Gaffney. 1988. Effective manning in the Orient. U.S. Department of Transportation, Maritime Administration, Washington, D.C. Report Number MA-RD-770-87052. March 15.

5

Legal and Regulatory Issues

The Coast Guard's authority to ensure the safe manning of merchant vessels has two aspects. First, the laws governing the regulation of U.S.-flag vessels are enforced by a certification and inspection process through which the agency sets minimum manning levels and ensures that vessels adhere to requirements over time. These statutes are effective impediments to the adoption of new technology. Outmoded and over-specific, they make it difficult for U.S. shipping companies to adopt the new technology and manning innovations available to their foreign competitors.

Second, a number of international agreements affect manning. These agreements, implemented by federal law, give the Coast Guard authority to inspect foreign-flag vessels entering U.S. ports to ensure that they adhere to international standards of operating safety. However, they do not provide a consistent, internationally accepted method for determining safe manning. The need for such a method will become more pressing with the worldwide adoption of new ship technology and innovative manning patterns.

An ideal international framework for determining safe manning would include (1) a universally accepted statement of principles setting forth functional manning requirements, and (2) an objective, analytical process for establishing minimum safe manning scales for vessels. Such a framework would help each vessel's flag state set manning levels. It could also be used by port states to ensure that all vessels entering their waters are safely manned. Internationally dictated manning scales are not desirable, however, since they would impose inappropriate standards on some ship operators, and would tend to freeze innovation for others.

74

SHIPPING AND CIVIL AVIATION:
CONTRASTING REGULATORY POLICIES

To put both issues in perspective, compare the domestic and international regulatory regimes of the maritime industry and the civil aviation industry. Discussions of vessel automation and smaller crews often focus on parallels between ships and commercial airliners, which are also increasingly automated and have also reduced their crews in recent years. For example, some concepts for highly automated vessels envision the bridge as a variation of the airliner's cockpit, with the watch officer monitoring all shipboard functions but rarely intervening in the steering or navigation of the ship.

Under the current maritime regulatory system, such comparisons may be more misleading than helpful. The two industries, as now constituted, are radically different, not only in the extent to which they have adopted new technology, but in the firmness and consistency—and international scope—of the laws and regulations that govern them. For the maritime industry, taking advantage of the new technology available to it would require a fundamental shift in its legal and regulatory foundations.

A comparison of the two industries illustrates the point:

• Navigation of airliners is directed by a mandatory traffic control system, which diminishes the human element in navigation decisions. Automated flight control systems further reduce the risk of human error. Ships, on the other hand, depend entirely on the attentiveness and skills of their crew members.

• Maintenance standards for airliners are higher than those for ships, and more strictly enforced. Federal aviation regulators oversee precisely specified and highly disciplined certification and maintenance procedures. In the maritime world, on the other hand, maintenance standards are highly variable, and federal regulation focuses on vessel performance rather than specified maintenance procedures.

• Working conditions and hours of work aboard aircraft are strictly limited by federal regulations and union work rules. Aircraft do not fly if the available crews have not had the specified opportunity to rest. Aboard merchant ships, current manning statutes as interpreted by federal courts set no upper limit on the hours a crew member may work.

• Requirements for training and qualification of airline flight crews are far more strict and standardized than those applied to ship's officers. Airlines benefit, for example, from the military training that most of their pilots have received, and from their own strictly certified and extremely rigorous training programs. Flight crews are certified for the specific aircraft type they fly, and are given rigorous physical examinations semiannually. Maritime licenses are renewed every five years, and permit the operation of nearly any type of vessel, without distinction. Aside from a color-blindness test, given with license-renewal examinations, no physical qualifications are imposed.

• The aircraft industry and its federal regulators spend generously on research and development to improve safety. The ship building and shipping industries, the Maritime Administration, and the Coast Guard have extremely small budgets for such research—particularly the human factors research that must undergird attempts to automate vessels.

Even in the civil aviation industry, the success of recent moves toward automation has been questioned (Hughes, 1989). Similarly, the safety of vessel automation and attendant crew reductions should not be taken for granted. A review of civil aviation regulatory policies, enforcement mechanisms and practices, and experience can provide constructive guidance in determining the degree of oversight required for efficient, safe use of new vessel technology.

THE STATUTORY BASIS FOR MANNING REGULATION

The laws governing the manning of merchant vessels have accreted over many years, beginning in the early years of this century.[1] Unlike more modern regulatory statutes (such as those governing commercial aircraft), they do not include a broad statement of policy or goals, according to which regulators may set standards. Instead, they prescribe a variety of specific manning practices, derived from the technology of the steamship. Notably, they require most shipboard workers to be divided into three watches (although most crew members on modern vessels do not stand watches); they forbid members of the deck and engine departments to cross departmental lines in their work; and they fail to effectively limit crew members' hours of work.

These provisions of the law, in their rigidity and specificity, leave little room for innovation, and discourage the adoption of new technology or more efficient manning practices. Furthermore, they place Coast Guard safety regulators in the awkward position of trying to accommodate new technology while adhering to the letter of manning laws that did not anticipate that technology.

The manning statute does not prohibit crew reductions. Crew levels aboard typical vessels could be lowered to perhaps 17 (from the low twenties today) without violating the law (see Appendix F). But neither efficiency

---

[1] The manning statutes are codified in Part F of Subtitle II of Title 46, United States Code (46 U.S.C. § 8101-9308), entitled "Manning of Vessels," Chapters 81, 83, 85, 87, 89, 91, and 93. The Coast Guard regulations that interpret and implement these laws are found in 46 CFR Part 15.

nor safety are served by the regulatory makeshift measures used by Coast Guard officials and companies to comply with the antiquated statute.

Some see the watch-standing and work-assignment requirements as protecting crew members from overwork by providing redundancy in the shipboard work force. It would be far more efficient to provide explicit protection against overwork and fatigue by authorizing regulatory limitations on hours of work, leaving other work rules to be determined by labor-management negotiation within the framework of a more rational regulatory regime.

Key Provisions of the Manning Statutes

Watch-standing Requirements

The division of deck and engine personnel into watches has been mandated by statute since 1915. The relevant statute (46 U.S.C. § 8104(d)) reads as follows:

> On a merchant vessel of more than 100 gross tons . . . the licensed individuals, sailors, coal passers, firemen, oilers, and water tenders shall be divided, when at sea, into at least 3 watches, and shall be kept on duty successively to perform ordinary work incident to the operation and management of the vessel.

This requirement has a strong effect on manning, because at least three persons must to be assigned to any position in one of these watch-standing categories. Aboard the typical ship of 30 or 50 years ago, powered by steam boilers and turbines that required round-the-clock attention, this requirement made sense. Today, with reliable, automated diesels, engine room personnel work during the day and sleep at night, except in emergencies. Aboard state-of-the-art European and Japanese ships, only the bridge watch—typically an officer or an officer and an unlicensed person—stands watches; everyone else works daytime shifts.

The watch-standing requirement of U.S. manning laws results in an inefficient use of personnel. Courts have generally interpreted this requirement strictly, to require that even day workers be divided into watches, so long as they fall in the job categories specified in the statute. (In a few cases, however, courts have held that certain day workers may be excepted from the watch-standing requirement; as explained below, this exception has permitted the formation of nonwatch-standing maintenance departments aboard some ships.)

Work Assignment Restrictions

Section 8104(e)(1) of Title 46, U.S.C., provides that a

> seaman may not be (A) engaged to work alternately in the deck and engine departments; or (B) required to work in the engine department if engaged for

deck department duty or required to work in the deck department if engaged
for engine department duty.

Again, this requirement, in its inflexibility, tends to discourage the adoption
of new technology.

Limitation of Hours of Work

Under 46 U.S.C. § 8104(d), a "licensed individual or seaman in the
deck or engine department may not be required to work more than 8 hours
in one day." Crew members may volunteer for overtime, provided they are
not coerced to do so. Courts have held that the existence of a collective
bargaining agreement specifying overtime standards makes overtime work
within those standards voluntary.

Thus, there is no effective limit on the hours a crew member may
work. This situation runs counter to the regulatory practice of any other
transportation industry. In practice, shipboard workers commonly work 10
to 12 hours a day, 7 days a week.

THE NEED TO MODERNIZE SAFETY REGULATION OF VESSELS

Individually, the provisions of the vessel manning statutes may have
been rational reactions to the circumstances that gave rise to them. Collectively, however, they deprive the Coast Guard and the shipping industry
of the flexibility needed to address manning of vessels in the light of new
technology, but do not provide adequately for safety.

As ship technology has advanced, the law's requirements have remained static. Coast Guard safety regulators and vessel operators have
adopted innovations within the limitations of the watch-standing requirement, the departmental cross-over restriction, and other provisions of the
manning statute, but have been unable to take a comprehensive and consistent approach to safety or the adoption of new technology.

The Maintenance Department:
A Regulatory Makeshift

An illustration of the problem is the development of the maintenance
department. As explained in Chapter 1, the Coast Guard has acquiesced
to the formation, aboard suitably equipped vessels, of nonwatch-standing
maintenance departments. The legal basis for this innovation can be found
in two court cases exempting certain personnel (those employed in positions not named in the watch-standing statute) from standing watch (see
Appendix F). In general, the Coast Guard has permitted crew members
engaged in routine maintenance, but not vessel operations, to be assigned
to maintenance departments.

The establishment of maintenance departments can be seen as an attempt to provide limited flexibility within the limits of an inflexible manning statute. The Coast Guard has made it clear, for example, that shipmasters may, at their discretion, use members of a maintenance department "to augment navigational or machinery-space watches should circumstances such as weather, mechanical failure, etc., require watch augmentation" (see Appendix F). When used to augment watches, however, maintenance persons become subject to the watch-keeping requirement.

Once a maintenance department is established, all personnel not required by the vessel's Certificate of Inspection (COI) can be engaged as maintenance persons, and thus relieved of watch duty. Engine maintenance persons required by the COI also can be assigned to the maintenance department. With approval of the Coast Guard, three of the six ABs (able-bodied seamen) normally required by the COI can also be converted to maintenance persons.

The legal basis for the maintenance department is regarded as tenuous (see Appendix F). A more coherent regulatory statute would help avoid such makeshift arrangements and place safety decisions on a firmer legal and analytical foundation.

THE INTERNATIONAL MANNING REGIME

In addition to the safety requirements set by domestic law, all ships must meet certain requirements set by international conventions. The existing international agreements, however, provide no clear framework for assessing manning issues.

Thus, the United States has limited options available to ensure safe manning of vessels that enter its ports. There is some anecdotal evidence that the more flagrant manning problems in U.S. waters are aboard foreign-flag ships (Bobb, 1989). The U.S. Coast Guard has authority to take corrective action in such cases, but lacks the analytical methods to exercise this authority fully.

International Agreements Affecting Manning

International Maritime Organization

International agreements regarding seagoing vessels are negotiated generally through the International Maritime Organization (IMO), a specialized agency of the United Nations. IMO's main objective is to facilitate cooperation among governments on technical matters affecting international shipping in the interests of safety and efficiency. IMO has special responsibilities for safety at sea and for preventing pollution by ships of the marine environment.

Much of IMO's work is devoted to producing and implementing international conventions. These fall into three general categories: marine safety, prevention of marine pollution, and liability and compensation.

Several conventions address most aspects of safety of life and property at sea and prevention of pollution from ships:

• The International Convention for the Safety of Life at Sea (SO-LAS), whose most recent version was adopted in 1974, is the fundamental international maritime safety agreement. It contains technical standards for safety surveys and certificates; subdivision and stability; machinery and electrical installations; fire protection, detection, and extinction; life-saving appliances; radiotelegraphy and radiotelephony; safety of navigation; carriage of grain and dangerous goods; and nuclear ships.

• The International Convention on Load Lines (1966) contains standards for calculating freeboard and assigning load lines of ships. The intent is to provide adequate reserve buoyancy for an intended voyage. The convention also addresses requirements for vessel strength and stability.

• The International Convention for the Prevention of Pollution from Ships (1973), modified by the Protocol of 1978 (MARPOL 73/78), contains standards for surveys and certificates, control of operational pollution, and minimizing pollution from tankers due to side and bottom damage.

• The Convention on the International Regulations for Preventing Collisions at Sea, COLREGS, (1972) provides an international scheme to enhance safety of navigation by preventing collisions between ships. COLREGS contains general navigation rules and regulations; steering and sailing rules; standards for lights, shapes, sound, and light signals; and interpretive rules.

• The Convention on the International Maritime Satellite Organization (INMARSAT) and its operating agreement, both of which entered into force in 1979, established an organization and operational procedures to improve maritime communications, thereby facilitating communications affecting the safety of life at sea, the efficiency of ship management, maritime public correspondence services, and radiotermination capabilities.

• The International Convention on Standards of Training, Certification and Watchkeeping for Seafarers (STCW), which entered into force in 1984 establishes international minimum standards for crew qualifications. This agreement (which the United States has not yet ratified) establishes minimum mandatory standards for persons in charge of navigational watches, engineering watches, and radio watch-keeping and maintenance, and sets out special requirements for personnel on tankers and standards for proficiency in survival craft.

These international conventions address nearly all aspects of marine safety: ship design, construction, equipment, operation, and the competency of crews.

IMO has not to date addressed specific manning levels. The STCW Convention specifies the qualifications of crew members and their watch-keeping practices, but is silent about crew levels. Many shipping states (including the United States) have requirements that exceed those of STCW in many respects.

The SOLAS Convention addresses manning in Chapter V, Regulation 13, by stating that, governments "undertake measures for the purpose of ensuring that, from the point of view of safety of life at sea, all ships shall be sufficiently and efficiently manned." Following up on work at the IMO that produced the STCW Convention, the IMO Assembly adopted Assembly resolution A.481(XII), "Principles of Safe Manning," in 1981. This resolution urges IMO member governments to ensure that each seagoing ship to which STCW applies carries a document specifying the vessel's minimum safe manning. The nonbinding resolution also contains recommended manning practices for bridge watches, mooring and unmooring, and other shipboard functions. It does not specify the levels of manning recommended, except in the case of bridge watches (in which case it refers to the provisions of STCW and SOLAS).

IMO Resolution A.647 (16), "IMO Guidelines on Management for the Safe Operation of Ships and for Pollution Prevention," was adopted October 19, 1989. It sets out suggested principles of safe management, which have manning implications. Each company, it says, should establish a formal safety and environmental protection policy, with necessary administrative staff. Vessels should be manned adequately for their trades by suitably qualified seafarers trained in safety and pollution prevention by appropriate emergency drills and other means. The resolution stresses that a vessel's master has the overriding onboard responsibility for safety and pollution prevention, and that companies should correct defects pointed out by masters. It also recommends attention to guidelines and requirements of classification societies and industry organizations.

The INMARSAT convention potentially affects manning by opening the way for dependable and convenient maritime satellite communications. Since INMARSAT terminals are more easily operated and considered more reliable than conventional radio sets, their introduction has led to calls for the elimination of radio officers on suitably equipped vessels. The automated Global Maritime Distress and Safety System, which operates through INMARSAT satellites, has lent further weight to these calls.

International Labour Organisation

The International Labour Organisation (ILO) is a United Nations body concerned with matters such as worker safety, compensation, and conditions of employment. The ILO Convention Concerning Minimum Standards in Merchant Ships (ILO 147) was adopted in 1976, and entered into force internationally on November 28, 1981. The United States ratified it in 1988, and it entered into force for this country in June 1989. Only 20 of the 150 ILO members have ratified the treaty. This convention requires that member nations implement safety standards including competency, work hours, manning, appropriate social security measures, shipboard employment conditions, and shipboard living arrangements.

This convention is similar to IMO resolution A.481(XII) (Principles of Safe Manning) in that contracting governments must set their own standards. The significance of the ILO convention, however, is that its provisions are mandatory (flag states must set national standards) and contain enforcement provisions (giving port states some enforcement authority over vessels entering their waters).

Article 4 of ILO 147 allows a port state to rectify any conditions that are clearly hazardous to safety, including insufficient manning. The U.S. Coast Guard provided guidance to field offices for enforcing ILO 147 in Commandant Instruction 16711.12, dated June 2, 1989.

Port State Control of Foreign-Flag Manning Practices

Port states have attempted to correct violations of international agreements by vessels visiting their waters through port state control provisions of international conventions. This practice of "port state control" of foreign-flag vessels includes enforcement measures regarding unsafe manning practices.

Coast Guard Captains of the Port (COTPs) have the authority to enforce safety requirements on foreign-flag vessels in U.S. ports. Under the provisions of the Port and Waterways Safety Act of 1972 (33 U.S.C. § 1223), as amended by the Port and Tanker Safety Act of 1978 (33 U.S.C. § 1228), and the basic manning statute (46 U.S.C. § 9101), the Coast Guard has clear authority to take action on unsafe manning practices. SOLAS Regulation 13, Chapter V, requires flag administrations to ensure that their ships are safely manned. Recently the IMO Maritime Safety Committee approved an amendment to this regulation to require that safe manning documents be issued by flag states to all vessels.

As a practical matter, the Coast Guard accepts manning levels established by flag states as evidence of safe manning on ships entering U.S. ports. However, the manning levels established by the various flag states, while theoretically based on IMO Resolution A-481, are not consistent. Difficulties arise when a flag state issues a safe manning document and a U.S. COTP believes the vessel is inadequately manned. To intervene the Coast Guard must be able to justify rejecting the flag state's manning assessment.

A similar situation faces other port states. For example, the Paris Memorandum of Understanding is an agreement of 14 Western European nations that establishes a coordinated port state inspection system. Its guidelines for accepting safe manning permit questioning of flag states' manning decisions. However, the members of the Paris agreement do not have a uniformly accepted method for assessment. The development of consistent manning criteria by flag states and consistent enforcement authority by port states requires a universally accepted analytical method for assessing safe manning. The IMO is the appropriate forum for resolving this matter.

FINDINGS

U.S. manning laws, in their specificity and rigidity, do not conform to modern regulatory practice, such as that in other transportation industries. There is no overall statement of congressional intent to be interpreted by regulators. Instead, there are specific manning requirements based on outmoded technology and operating practices. These requirements—notably the division of crew members into three watches, and the prohibition of departmental crossovers—provide inadequate protection of workers and hamper the safe and efficient use of new technology.

As crew levels decline, these laws deprive the maritime industry of the flexibility needed to best utilize the crew members assigned. The Coast Guard, in an effort to permit technical innovation within the letter of the manning laws, has adopted innovations such as the shipboard maintenance department, which may be subject to challenge under differing legal interpretations.

While the Coast Guard has the authority to examine manning levels for foreign vessels entering U.S. waters and take exception where appropriate, a more pragmatic approach would be to address this issue internationally. Current international agreements already contain certain accepted principles of safe manning. What is needed is an internationally accepted analytical method for establishing and assessing minimum safe manning. The United States should develop such a method for use domestically and propose it at IMO for international acceptance. Chapter 4 discusses the utility of such a method, and describes a committee-developed task analysis model that could form the basis of such a widely applicable assessment method.

REFERENCES

Alaska Oil Spill Commission. 1990. Spill: The Wreck of the Exxon Valdez, Implications
    for Safe Marine Transportation. Anchorage: Alaska Oil Spill Commission. January.
Bobb, John. 1989. Statement of the International Organization of Masters, Mates, and Pilots
    on manning before the Marine Board of the National Research Council, Washington,
    D.C. September 14.
Hughes, David. 1989. Glass cockpit study reveals human factors problems. Aviation Week
    and Space Technology. August 7.
Lloyd's Register of Shipping. Provisional rules for the classification of shipborne navigational
    equipment. London. September.

6

Conclusions and Recommendations

SAFETY EXPERIENCE WITH SMALLER CREWS

Analysis of national and worldwide maritime safety data supports the conclusion that the number of vessel casualties and personnel injuries has declined steadily over the past two decades. During the same period, average crew sizes have been substantially reduced. In gathering and analyzing worldwide maritime safety data, the committee was unable to establish a causal relationship between manning levels and safety.

Available data on maritime safety are inadequate to support firm judgments about the contributions of various factors, such as crew levels, to safety. A worldwide effort is needed to standardize, gather, and evaluate safety data in order to identify trends and provide the technical basis for constructive management of maritime safety. The following developments are needed worldwide:

- standardization of information about casualties, their causes, and their consequences;
- collection of information about the exposure of ships to casualties, including data tabulated on the basis of ton-miles and numbers of port calls; and
- collection of comprehensive data, including size and organization of crews, on all vessels.

RECOMMENDATION: The U.S. Department of Transportation, through the Coast Guard, should organize and lead a broad-based effort (international in scope) to gather, standardize, evaluate, and disseminate maritime safety data.

TECHNOLOGY AND INNOVATION

The pace of change continues. Foreign-flag fleets have set the pace at which new technologies are being adopted on ships. They have well planned, methodical programs to use technology effectively and safely, bringing crew levels in some cases down to the low teens. Innovation in the U.S. fleet is essential to competition. The way in which innovation is implemented will determine whether safety is helped or hindered. Above all, the U.S. fleet should leverage other countries' experience with their systematic programs in developing its own reduced crew ships of the future.

Progress can be achieved only by close cooperation among all interested parties, including ship operators, the seagoing work force, and the industry's safety and economic regulators. This collaborative effort should encompass training, research, evaluation and dissemination of information on international developments, and pilot programs under the U.S. flag. Government can serve as a catalyst in this effort, but the industry itself (including operators and labor) will need to lead.

RECOMMENDATION: The industry, with the aid of the U.S. Department of Transportation, should implement a program to demonstrate the safety of changes in the crewing of ships. This program would have three elements:

1. a program focusing on (1) research oriented toward innovation in the application of new technology; (2) efforts to understand and apply foreign experience; and (3) research to determine how human factors, such as fatigue and stress, affect maritime safety;
2. a program to demonstrate and evaluate U.S.-flag ships of the future, leveraging other nations' experiences with ship of the future programs; and
3. a government-industry-labor forum to oversee developments in the manning of ships.

As a first step, the Department of Transportation should call a meeting of senior executives of ship operating companies and maritime labor unions to determine the extent of interest in this initiative and to discuss its leadership. An important outcome of this process will be the definition of specific developments needed in training programs and maritime licensing.

HUMAN FACTORS AND SAFETY CERTIFICATION

The introduction of new technology should consider ships as sociotechnical systems, consisting of personnel, technology, organizational structures, and an external environment. Change in any of these four subsystems should suggest appropriate changes in the others.

New vessel technology coupled with appropriate training, organizational innovations, and ergonomic design can enhance safety. For example, these approaches can reduce potential problems of stress, fatigue, and boredom.

The U.S. Coast Guard and other national ship safety administrations do not presently have the necessary human factors analysis methods to make solid certification decisions on minimum safe manning for highly automated ships.

In establishing safe crew levels, government and industry need to consider demands on the crews on different vessels, taking into account specialized technologies, type of service, skills required, and quality of management. Formal analytical methods need to be incorporated into the establishment of safe crew levels and the consequent issuance of Certificates of Inspection (COIs). Lack of an analytical approach has led to inconsistent COI determinations and has made it difficult for the Coast Guard to exercise its port state control authorities.

RECOMMENDATION: The Coast Guard should institute formal analytical methods, such as the functional analysis approach suggested in Chapter 4, in making manning decisions.

RECOMMENDATION: In the vessel certification process for vessels employing new manning concepts, each operator should conduct a thorough assessment of shipboard functions and tasks required by the particular vessel and should submit a functional analysis (with specified crew numbers and structure, skills and training, voyage profiles, and operational and maintenance plans) to the Coast Guard for approval. Upon conditional approval by the Coast Guard, vessels should be subjected to such sea trials as the Coast Guard deems appropriate, with logs of crew activities. Data from the trials should be used to validate the results obtained from the model.

TRAINING AND LICENSING

The skills needed to operate ships are changing with advances in technology. Lines dividing deck and engine departments are fading, along with the need for engine room watch-keeping. The importance of individual and team skills is increasing as crews are reduced. These changes need to be reflected in training programs and licensing requirements.

Training programs must reflect not only technical skills required, but subjects such as management of personnel and communications. Licensing requirements must become more specialized to reflect the differences in vessel type and service and to require periodic recertification of skills to ensure that crew members develop and retain necessary qualifications. The certification and licensing of general purpose ratings, dual-qualified officers and watch officers should be established to reflect the changing ship organizational structure.

LEGAL AND REGULATORY ISSUES

While U.S. manning laws have not been a major impediment to crew reduction aboard U.S.-flag vessels to date, they have led to needless inefficiency and complexity and to unwarranted obstacles to most effective manning that realizes the benefits of new ship operating technology. Furthermore, it is clear that these statutes will effectively prohibit manning reductions below current levels regardless of the opportunities offered by technology, such as those evident in state-of-the-art foreign-flag vessels. Thus, while not a major problem in the past, these statutes will block innovation and competitiveness in the future.

Even more important, existing manning laws do not directly address safety. They do not have a clear underlying safety intent, and therefore inhibit innovation without affording real gain in safety. The little guidance available is informal and administrative.

RECOMMENDATION: The manning laws of the United States should be modernized in line with the following objectives:

• Incorporate a statement of congressional intent linking vessel manning and safety.

• Remove unwarranted barriers to innovation (such as requirements for three watches where impractical or not needed).

• Establish a clear federal role in reviewing the safety of vessel manning practices by (1) authorizing the overhaul of the licensing system; (2) ratifying the International Convention on Standards of Training, Certification and Watchkeeping for Seafarers, (3) establishing a uniform COI issuance process; and (4) reviewing the need for work-hour limitations that provide real protection of crew members' health and environmental safety.

Appendix A

Biographies of Committee Members

RICHARD T. SOPER, appointed chairman in January 1990, was until April 1990, Chairman of the American Bureau of Shipping, a leading international ship classification society. He is an articulate proponent of innovation in the maritime industries and in operating safety. Mr. Soper earned his B.S. degree in 1955 through combined study at the Massachusetts Maritime Academy and Harvard University. He has worked in international shipping for more than 30 years, gaining experience in marine vessel operations and marine insurance. His work prior to graduation was as a licensed deck officer and port captain for American Export Lines. After graduation he was employed by Kemper Insurance in several managerial positions, Assistant to the Vice President of Engineering, Chief Hull Underwriter, and Assistant Manager of the Marine Insurance Division. In 1962, he joined Sea-Land Service, Inc., serving as Manager, Vessel Operations, and later as Assistant Director of Marine Operations. Following a period (1966-1969) as Executive Vice President of Columbus Line, Inc., Mr Soper rejoined Sea-Land where he rose to Executive Vice President. Mr. Soper has served on the Marine Board and on its Committee on Requirements for a Ship Operation Research Program.

WILLIAM M. BENKERT, chairman until his death in December 1989, received his B.S. degree in marine engineering from the U.S. Coast Guard Academy in 1943. His Coast Guard career was composed of extensive sea duty and marine safety assignments. He was captain of the icebreaker *Eastwind* on arctic and antarctic assignments, commanded the Marine

Inspection Office in New York, and was Chief of the Headquarters Office of Merchant Marine Safety. After retiring from the Coast Guard, he served as President of the American Institute of Merchant Shipping. He was a member of several professional societies, was a past member of the Maritime Transportation Research Board and the Marine Board, and served on several NRC committees. He chaired Marine Board committees on marine vapor control and on removal of offshore platforms.

JOHN V. CAFFREY is Manager, Maritime Relations, Mobil Oil Corporation, Marine Transportation Department. He has general oversight of safety, security, and internal affairs for Mobil's domestic and international fleets and develops policy positions on legislative and regulatory shipping matters. He entered the marine industry as an unlicensed seaman aboard United Fruit Lines vessels. He served at sea in all deck capacities, advancing to command as master (a license he still holds) before joining the U.S. Coast Guard. He served 27 years in the Coast Guard, ashore and afloat, with extensive service in the office of Merchant Marine Safety. Recent assignments included Chief Officer of Merchant Vessel Personnel, and Deputy Chief, Office of Merchant Marine Safety. He serves on the Training Committee of the American Institute of Merchant Shipping, the General Purposes Committee of the Oil Companies International Marine Forum, the National Executive Committee of the Council of American Master Mariners. He is a member and past Chairman of the National Safety Council's Marine Section. Captain Caffrey was a member of the NRC Marine Board Committee on Effective Manning in 1983-1984.

MICHAEL DENNY is an industrial psychologist specializing in the human factors design of automated work systems. He is a Senior Systems Designer for the Grumman Corporation's Data Systems Division. He received B.S., M.A. and Ph.D. degrees in experimental psychology from Michigan State University, where he was a National Science Foundation fellow. As assistant professor of psychology, he received the MSU Foundation Faculty Award. He later became project manager and branch manager for Ship Analytics, Inc., where he led several large programs focusing on ship operations research and the restructuring of vessel crews and their management. These efforts were aimed at improving work efficiency and achieving optimal reduced manning. His ship operations research studies included experiments at the U.S. government's Computer Aided Operations Research Facility (CAORF) at Kings Point, New York, a large ship-handling simulator facility. He made vessel manning and management studies for two major vessel operating companies and the U.S. Navy, which formed the basis for successful fleetwide manning reductions and restructuring. These included both existing vessels and proposed new vessel designs, in which the entire vessel-crew system could be optimized for cost and safety.

WILLIAM D. EGLINTON is Director of Vocational Training at the Seafarers Harry Lundeberg School of Seamanship, operated by the Seafarers International Union. He received a B.S. degree in technology and management from the University of Maryland, graduated from the Calhoon Marine Engineers Beneficial Association School. After serving as a licensed officer in the U.S. merchant marine, he became an engineering instructor at the Harry Lundeberg School, then head of the Engineering Department, before assuming his present post. He personally trained the initial crews of several U.S. merchant vessels and developed courses on diesel engines and other engineering systems. He is the author of the *Marine Engineroom Blue Book* and the *Study Guide for Third and Second Assistant Engineers* (Cornell Maritime Press).

ROBERT ELSENSOHN is Director of the Maritime Institute of Technology and Graduate Studies (MITAGS), operated by the International Organization of Masters, Mates and Pilots (IOMMP). He graduated from the U.S. Maritime Services Officers School. He holds numerous certifications for unlicensed and licensed maritime skills and grades, including advanced training in shiphandling from MITAGS. During World War II, Captain Elsensohn served as an unlicensed seaman in various U.S. ocean vessels. He has served in positions of increasing responsibility, including seagoing deck officer, on many ship types. He has served as President of Columbia River Bar Pilots, Vice President-Pilotage of the International Organization of Masters, Mates and Pilots (IOMMP), President and Chief Executive Officer of the Columbia Navigation Corporation, and Pilot Commissioner of the state of Oregon. In his present position as Director of MITAGS, he supervises all operations, including courses on the handling of conventional dry and liquid cargoes and hazardous commodities, such as liquefied natural gas, petroleum gas, and ammonia. Captain Elsensohn is a member of the IOMMP and the American Pilots Association, and is a fellow of the Nautical Institute.

MARTHA GRABOWSKI is Research Assistant Professor in the Department of Decision Sciences and Engineering Systems at Rennselaer Polytechnic Institute and is Assistant Professor of Business at LeMoyne College in Syracuse, New York. She received a B.S. degree in Marine Transportation from the U.S. Merchant Marine Academy, and M.S., M.B.A., and Ph.D. degrees from Rennselaer Polytechnic Institute. She served as a licensed deck officer on a liquefied natural gas tanker for El Paso Marine Company and on conventional tankers for Exxon and Hvide Shipping, and was commissioned a lieutenant commander in the U.S. Naval Reserve. She is Manager of Expert Systems Applications for General Electric Company, where she received management awards in 1984 and 1987 for leadership in developing expert systems. Her research is supported by the U.S. Maritime Administration, and she is at present developing a Shipboard Piloting Expert System (SPES) and investigating the effects of smaller shipboard crews and advanced technology on maritime safety, methods for streamlined development of expert systems, and the organizational impact of expert systems.

HAL W. HENDRICK is professor and dean, College of Systems Science, University of Denver. His expertise is in industrial and organizational psychology, behavioral science, and human factors. Dr. Hendrick has done extensive research in leadership, managerial decision making, individual differences and performance, organizational assessment and development, and human factors. Former academic positions have included Professor and Director of the Institute of Safety and Systems Management, University of Southern California, and positions on the faculty of the U.S. Air Force Academy. Dr. Hendrick is a fellow of the Human Factors Society and the American Psychological Association. Dr. Hendrick received a B.A. (psychology) from Ohio Wesleyan University and M.S. (human factors) and Ph.D. (industrial psychology) degrees from Purdue University.

FRANK J. IAROSSI was until April 1990 President of Exxon Shipping Company and is now Chairman of the American Bureau of Shipping. He received his B.S. degree in Marine Engineering from the U.S. Coast Guard Academy, M.S. degree in Naval Architecture and Mechanical Engineering from the University of Michigan, and M.B.A. degree from New York University. He joined Exxon International Company in 1968 in the research and development division, and was manager of the Far East Tanker Construction Program in Kobe, Japan during the building of Exxon's fleet of very large tankers in the early 1970s. He later served as a marine operations senior advisor for Exxon. He is a member of the Society of Naval Architects and Marine Engineers, a director of the American Institute of Merchant Shipping, past chairman of the Marine Transportation Committee of the American Petroleum Institute, and a member of the Board of Managers of the American Bureau of Shipping.

Since 1967, **JEROME E. JOSEPH** has served as Executive Vice President for District 2 of the Marine Engineers Beneficial Association—Associated Maritime Officers. He received a B.S. degree from the U.S. Merchant Marine Academy at Kings Point, New York. He then sailed as deck officer aboard U.S. merchant vessels for four years before becoming Assistant Operations Manager for a U.S.-flag steamship company. Mr. Joseph has also served as president of the Propeller Club of the United States, Port of New York. He is a member of the Executive Committee of the Propeller Club of the United States, the College Council, the State University of

New York Maritime College, the Kings Point Fund, the Chairman Walter Jones' Kitchen Cabinet, the New York City Office of Collective Bargaining, and the Navy League.

EUGENE M. KELLY was until April 1990 Vice President, Engineering, for Central Gulf Lines, a U.S.-flag ship operating company. He received a B.S. degree in Marine Engineering from the U.S. Coast Guard Academy, and an M.S. degree in naval architecture, marine engineering, and mechanical engineering from the University of Michigan. He served in the Coast Guard as a seagoing deck and engineering officer, and later as staff officer in the Merchant Marine Technical Office at Coast Guard Headquarters. While with the Coast Guard, he served in London with the U.S. delegation to the 1969 International Maritime Organization Conference on Tonnage Measurement. Following this, Mr. Kelly served in naval architecture positions in the Tanker Department of Exxon International Company and the Marine Department of Continental Oil Company. He joined Sea-Land Service, Inc. in 1977, and served as Vice President of Fleet Engineering, Vice President and General Manager of Sea Readiness, Inc., Director of Marine Engineering, Regional Manager Fleet Engineering/Atlantic, Chief Naval Architect, and Group Vice President, Marine Operations and Engineering.

STEPHEN F. SCHMIDT is Vice President of Marine Operations for American President Lines (APL), where he has overall responsibility for the APL fleet of 23 U.S.-flag containerships, plus various foreign-flag feeder vessels. He received a B.S. degree in marine transportation from the U.S. Merchant Marine Academy, then sailed as 3rd and 2nd officer aboard U.S. merchant vessels for three years before returning ashore, where he had various management positions for Sea-Land Service in the United States and Europe. After moving to APL, he was Director of Terminal Operations, Vice President of Asia, and Vice President of Logistics for APL and American President Intermodal before assuming his present position.

Appendix B
Survey of Classification Societies
and Foreign Governments

From the outset, the committee acknowledged that the requests for reduced manning on U.S. merchant ships were not unique. Foreign-flag vessels operating worldwide and entering U.S. waters were operating with noticeably fewer crew members along the same trade routes as U.S.-flag vessels. Individual foreign governments and international organizations such as the International Labor Organization (ILO) and the International Maritime Organization (IMO) had been similarly obliged to address shipboard manning levels while considering the safety consequences of increasing shipboard automation capabilities, sustaining the international competitiveness of the national flag fleet, preventing the "flagging out" of ships from high cost national fleets to lower cost "offshore registries," and searching for remedies to a shortage of labor in the national merchant marine.

Occasionally, reports of smaller crew experiments reached the U.S. shipping industry audience via industry associations or other private organizations overseas. Those reports were often abbreviated in such a way that the perspective of the official classification societies and the national maritime authorities were unavailable. Therefore, while the final results of the experiments may have been reported to a wide American audience, the process by which the decisions had been taken to bring the experiment to a successful conclusion were less well documented.

The committee decided to initiate direct inquiries to a number of official organizations about how the requests for smaller crews coming from ship operators were being handled. The objective of the effort was to determine what criteria had been developed to assess the safety aspects of reduced manning levels.

In March 1989, a letter questionnaire was sent to 17 organizations in Britain, Western Europe, and Japan requesting comments on issues of crew requirements for smaller crew requests, vessel requirements for smaller crew requests, and the safety performance of vessels operating with smaller crews. The letter and accompanying questionnaire are attached.

RESULTS OF SURVEY

Thirteen replies were received. The IMO secretariat provided several documents, five classification societies sent informative replies, and seven foreign government maritime authorities sent copies of domestic regulations and policy documents on shipboard manning, including the issues of smaller crews. The bibliography of replies and documents provided is attached.

The results showed that the classification societies generally deferred to official government authorities in determining manning levels. None of the classification societies surveyed has authority to determine the manning of a vessel. All five are active in establishing requirements for ship design and construction requirements—the traditional purview of the classification society—and have extended their activities into developing specialized hardware and vessel layout requirements to enable the vessel to be classified for unattended engine room operations or reduced manning of bridge watches.

The maritime authorities' replies confirmed that the authorities reserve the setting of merchant ship crew numbers, qualifications, and training. Smaller crew ships and reduced manning requests are increasingly common. The maritime authority replies regarding specialized vessel requirements for smaller crew requests reflect the close relationships between the official maritime authorities and the classification societies in the maritime industry. (This degree of symbiosis in a government organization delegating technical oversight to a private organization may be unique to the merchant marine.) All seven maritime authorities indicated that they had developed criteria for considering vessel manning, including reduced manning requests. These criteria include technical features of vessel design and construction typically overseen by classification societies.

Maritime authorities use criteria for reduced manning levels from two sources, the International Maritime Organization conventions and their own domestic regulations. No IMO convention specifically establishes safe manning standards, but five of seven national authorities use the Principles of Safe Manning (resolution A.481 [XII], adopted November 19, 1981), which are elaborated in the International Convention on Standards of Training, Certification and Watchkeeping for Seafarers, 1978 (1978 STCW

Convention). These principles are not aimed at achieving any fixed crew size, but set out overall functional criteria that must be sustained on any vessel in service, regardless of the number of seafarers in the crew.

The replies indicate a changing definition of the ship's officers and seamen's duties, away from the traditional division into deck and engineering departments still required by U.S. law. Two national authorities provided copies of national merchant marine personnel laws and regulations, showing that they have been substantively amended or completely restructured within the past decade, specifically in response to pressure from fleet owners and favorable results of smaller crew ship experiments. Norway established new regulations in 1987, for example, and Sweden's new standards date from 1988. The Dutch authority's reply indicates a deliberate four-stage transition from a traditional crew organization to what they consider a smaller basic crew, with restructured crew qualifications.

The unanimous response to the questions on vessel casualties was that there had been none that could be related to the introduction of smaller crews on existing or new ships. Three national authorities even volunteered that the operation of smaller crew vessels improved safety, because crew members were more experienced, better trained, and individually more aware of the need to work safely than was the case in traditionally manned vessels.

NATIONAL RESEARCH COUNCIL
COMMISSION ON ENGINEERING AND TECHNICAL SYSTEMS
2101 Constitution Avenue   Washington, D.C. 20418

MARINE BOARD

OFFICE LOCATION:
Georgetown Facility
Room HA 250
2001 Wisconsin Avenue, N.W.
Telephone: (202) 334-3119
Telefax: (202) 334-2620

SMALLER CREWS SURVEY LETTER
(Sent to Classification Societies/National Authorities)

March 6, 1989
MB-89-187

Dear _____:

In the United States, as in other maritime nations, ship owners are
operating their vessels with fewer crew, relying more on automation
technologies and planned ship maintenance programs than was the case ten years
ago. The United States Coast Guard, which is responsible for all U.S.
merchant vessel safety, must decide whether each vessel can operate safely
with a given number of people. At the Coast Guard's request, the Marine Board
of the National Research Council is assessing the effect of smaller crews on
maritime safety. Our aim is to advise the U.S. Coast Guard on how to weigh
the requests made of them for reduced manning, rather than to spell out what
number of crew members makes a ship safe.

The enclosed committee roster demonstrates that we have involved broad
representation from the American maritime community to study what changes may
be needed to ensure that ships and crews continue to sail safely. Our
committee's approach to examining these factors is presented in the enclosed
Statement of Task. Our work should be finished by year's end with a public
report to be released thereafter.

We request your assistance in our task. We want to learn how similar
organizations, such as yours, have approached the introduction of smaller
crews on new and existing merchant vessels. Our own deliberations will be
improved by the opportunity to learn how you and your colleagues considered
the same question and what factors you evaluated in making your decision on
the matter.

You can be most helpful by answering the enclosed list of questions. Any
remarks you may offer on the safety of smaller crews, in addition to the
questions, would also be helpful; so would references that may lead us to
other efforts, such as our own, underway on behalf of ship operators,
classification societies, or national authorities.

*The National Research Council is the principal operating agency of the National Academy of Sciences and the National Academy of Engineering
to serve government and other organizations*

2

Thank you in advance for your assistance. Your response will be most helpful if received by April 21, 1989. I will be pleased to provide you with the final report of this project early next year. Please direct your responses to:

Mr. Charles A. Bookman, Director
Marine Board, HA 250
National Research Council
2101 Constitution Avenue
Washington, DC 20418

Attn: Committee on the Effect of Smaller Crews
on Maritime Safety

Sincerely,

W.M. Benkert
Committee Chairman

WMB/LAM:GG

Enclosures (4)
Survey Questions
Statement of Task
Committee Roster
Marine Board Brochure

SURVEY OF INTERNATIONAL CLASSIFICATION SOCIETIES

QUESTIONS ON SAFETY OF SMALLER CREWS
Prepared by

Committee on the Effect of Smaller Crews on Maritime Safety
Marine Board
National Research Council
March 3, 1989

for

National Shipping Organizations and International Classification Societies

A. Consideration of Reduced Manning Levels

> Has your organization considered approving, on a permanent or temporary basis, manning levels below a total complement of 16 for oceangoing merchant vessels?
>
> If so, please name the vessels and tell us the number of crew members you approved for each vessel.
>
> Please describe the crew license requirements, on a permanent or temporary basis, and crew skill qualifications you required when approving this smaller crew.

B. Criteria for Reduced Manning Levels

> Does your organization have published criteria or guidelines regarding approval of reduced manning? Are criteria different for new and existing vessels?
>
> What vessel features, design requirements, or operational performance requirements did you consider important to your decision to approve reduced manning levels? Similarly, are there any features or requirements that would lead you to disapprove reduced manning for a specific vessel?
>
> What criteria have you devised to judge the overall safety of the vessel when operated at the reduced manning level?

Did your organization authorize a trial operational period for the vessel, to demonstrate safe performance with the smaller crew? If so, was it a prelude to permanent approval of the smaller crew? How did you evaluate the trial period? Please elaborate.

C. Experience of Vessels with Smaller Crews

Does your organization have quantitative data regarding the relationship between crew complement and vessel safety or personnel safety?

Has any vessel approved for operation with fewer than 16 crew members been involved in a major operating casualty; e.g., collision, grounding, sinking, or major machinery failure? Was the smaller number of crew on board a factor in either causing or responding to the casualty emergency? Please provide supporting information.

Has your organization developed a position regarding the relationship between manning level and vessel safety or personnel safety?

Please send your replies to:

Mr. Charles A. Bookman, Director
Marine Board, HA 250
National Research Council
2101 Constitution Avenue
Washington, DC 20418
Attn: Committee on the Effect of
    Smaller Crews on Maritime Safety

Thank you for your assistance.

Committee on the Effect of Smaller Crews
on Maritime Safety
1989 Survey of Classification Societies
and
National Maritime Authorities

On March 6, 1989, the committee sent a letter questionnaire to 17 classification societies and foreign national authorities. The Marine Board received these 13 replies.

Reply from International Maritime Organization

1. International Maritime Organization, dated March 22, 1989, prepared by Y. Sasamura, Assistant Secretary General, Director, Maritime Safety Division, with enclosures:

    A. IMO Resolution A. 481(XII), principles of safe manning
    B. STCW Regulation II/1, paragraph 9 lookout,
    C. COLREG Rule 5, lookout
    D. SOLAS Regulation 13, manning.

Replies from Classification Societies

2. Det norske Veritas, dated April 26, 1989, prepared by Tor-Christian Mathiesen, Head of Division Ship and Offshore, with enclosures:

    A. Introduction to Det Norske Veritas, established 1864. Rules for Nautical Safety, Naut-A, Naut-B, Naut-C, July 1986 and Tentative Rules for One-Man Bridge Operation in Ocean Areas and Coastal Waters (W1-OC):
    B.1. Philosophy on manning of ships;
    B.2. Methodology used in determining manning levels;
    B.3. DnV's approach for establishing technical standards in relation to manpower;
    B.4. Answers to questions on safety of smaller crews.

3. Lloyd's Register, dated April 5, 1989, prepared by J. G. Beaumont, Chief Ship Surveyor, no enclosures.

4. Registro Italiano Navale, dated April 5, 1989, prepared by office of the Direzione Generale, no enclosures.

5. Bureau Veritas, dated April 6, 1989, prepared by Managing Director, Marine Branch, no enclosures.

6. Nippon Kaiji Kyokai, dated April 17, 1989, prepared by K. Shiraishi, General Manager, Machinery Department, with enclosures:

A. Modernized ships (1 page),

B. Modernized ships of type 2 (16 crew members) as of February 1989.

7. American Bureau of Shipping, dated November 30, 1989, prepared by Richard T. Soper, Chairman and President, no enclosures.

Replies from National Authorities

8. Netherlands Ministerie van Verkeer en Waterstaat, Directoraat-Generaal Scheepvaart en Maritieme Zaken, dated April 17, 1989, prepared by Mr. R. van der Poel, the Head of the Ship's Safety Department, on behalf of the Head of Shipping Inspection, no enclosures.

9. Canadian Coast Guard, dated April 18, 1989, prepared by M. J. Hubbard, Director General Ship Safety Branch, with enclosures:

A. Canada Shipping Act, Chapter 1481, ship's deck watch regulations. Regulations respecting the establishment of deck watches and the number and qualifications of navigational personnel on ships, with 6 amendments.

B. Canada Shipping Act Chapter 1466, Safe manning regulations. Regulations respecting the manning of steamships, with two amendments.

10. Der Bundesminister fur Verkehr (in German), dated April 18, 1989 prepared by Herr Hapke (no first name given). Translated by NRC staff member Ms. Hanu, with enclosure:

A. Excerpt (1 page) of the Abweichungen von der Regelbesatzung (in German, not translated).

11. Sjofartsdirektoratet (Norwegian Maritime Directorate), dated April 13, 1989 prepared by Emil Jansen, Deputy Director General of Shipping and Navigation. Please direct inquiries however to Principal Surveyor A Bornes, with enclosures:

A. The regulations of March 17, 1987 concerning the manning of Norwegian ships.

B. The regulations of July 1, 1987 concerning qualifications required for personnel on Norwegian ships for whom a certificate of competency is not required.

C. The Act of June 5, 1981, No. 42, concerning certification of personnel on Norwegian ships, drilling units and other mobile offshore installations, with appurtenant regulations (47 pages) dated December 11, 1981 concerning:

- certificates of competency for masters and mates,

- qualifications required for masters of passenger ships of less than 25 gross register tons,
- minimum age, etc. for masters of certain engine-propelled vessels of less than 25 gross register tons,
- certificates of competency for marine engineer officers,
- certificates of competency as marine electro-automation officer,
- certificates of competency for marine cooks (fishing), marine chief cooks and marine catering officers, and
- certificates of competency for personnel on drilling units and other mobile offshore installations.

D. Regulations of January 14, 1985 concerning special requirements with regard to training and qualifications for personnel on tankers.

12. U.K. Department of Transport Marine Directorate, dated April 13, 1989, prepared by Captain J. Groves, Nautical Surveyor, with enclosures:

A. Department of Transport application for safe manning certificate (revised 1987),

B. Safe manning certificate for United Kingdom registered seagoing ship (revised 1987),

C. Merchant Shipping Notice No. M1178, manning of merchant ships registered in the United Kingdom.

13. Sjofartsverket Sjofartsinspektionen (Swedish authority), dated April 24, 1989, prepared by Kjell Eliasson, of the Fartygsoperativa sektionen, Bemanning, with enclosures:

A. Ship Safety Act (1988:49) Chapter 5—Manning of Ships,

B. Ship Safety Ordinance (1988:594) Sections 1 through 20.

14. Danish Maritime Authority, dated June 19, 1989, prepared by T. R. Funder, Director General, with enclosure:

June 16, 1989, reply to questionnaire on safety of smaller crews.

Appendix C

Information from Labor Unions

COMMITTEE ON THE EFFECTS OF SMALLER CREWS
ON MARITIME SAFETY
September 14, 1989
Maritime Labor Perspective on Safety of Smaller Crews

In 1989, the discussion of how maritime industry practices might affect mariners' performance became very public. Both the National Transportation Safety Board and the U.S. Congress turned to issues of crews, extended work schedules, and the fatigue, stress, and degraded performance that might result. The attention followed vessel casualties where operator error attributed to fatigue was considered a possible contributing cause of the casualty. Public statements, occasionally anecdotal, had been made directly relating vessel safety to the smaller crews' working situation.

The chairman, after consulting with three committee members who are labor organization members, extended an open invitation to 19 labor organizations to participate in a structured discussion of the labor perspective of the changes brought by shipboard manning reductions. Chairman Benkert stated that, in his opinion, the work conducted to date on the topic of vessel automation and reduced crews had been based on studying the technological advancement involved, with less attention being paid to the human consequences, other than the numerical changes in crew size.

Nine organizations—representing deck officers, marine engineers, radio electronics officers, sailors, and pilots—accepted the invitation to speak

104

at the meeting or bring information to the attention of the committee. In addition, guests from the National Transportation Safety Board and the U.S. Maritime Administration Office of Labor and Training submitted information and attended this session.

Presenters

1. George Quick (GQ), Association of Maryland Pilots; Masters, Mates and Pilots.

2. Brian Hope (BH), Association of Maryland Pilots; Masters, Mates and Pilots, and member of the Maryland State Board of Licensing.

3. Don Dishinger (DD), Technical Director, Radio Electronics Officers' Union.

4. John Hillman (JH), Board of Governors, Exxon Seamen's Union.

5. Augie Tellez (AT), Vice President, Seafarers International Union of North America, AFL-CIO.

6. Daniel O'Shea (DO), Alliance of Independent Maritime Organizations.

7. John Bobb (JB), Academic Director of the Maritime Institute of Technology and Graduate Studies, International Organization of Masters, Mates and Pilots.

8. Richard Berger (RB), Director of Research and Development, Marine Engineers Beneficial Association/National Maritime Union (MEBA 1/NMU, AFL-CIO).

9. John Pitts (JP), Atlantic Maritime Employees Union.

10. Talmadge Simpkins (TS), Executive Director, AFL-CIO Maritime Committee.

Excerpts from Speakers' Points Of Concern

All speakers expressed concerns regarding safety, fatigue, and the validity of the economic savings attributed to the use of smaller crews. Additionally, they addressed the substance and methods of the NRC study itself and offered suggestions for the committee to use in exploring the unstudied problems of mariners working on reduced crew ships.

Excerpts from the speakers remarks or from their prepared statements follow.

INADEQUATE LOOKOUT

(GQ) 2-man watches leave nobody to act as lookout. One person cannot both steer and act as lookout.

(JH) With only two ABs on a watch, you cannot maintain a proper lookout when you change from lookout to helmsman.

POOR HELMSMAN

(GQ) Shoreside managements have cut back on the vessel manning to the point where vessels are entering our pilotage waters without a helmsman, with only one AB and one officer on watch.

(BH) Because the wheel is so commonly on autopilot, the helmsman gets no experience steering by hand, and the person at the wheel may not know how to steer.

CREW STANDARDS GENERALLY

(AT) We still need "trained and experienced humans who can recognize, act on and solve a problem long before automated devices are capable of detecting any incipient dangers."

(RB) Crewing standards and vessel maintenance are being too casually treated.

LANGUAGE DIFFICULTY

(BH) People seem more isolated, especially on the multinational, multilanguage crews. For example, it is not unusual for an English-speaking officer to approach a pilot with relief as a fellow English-speaker.

(GQ) Rarely, a crew will speak no English at all, which can be difficult for the pilot. Occasionally, you find that the officers and the crew have no common language, or speak only through onboard foremen/interpreters.

COMPLEX AUTOPILOTS

(GQ) These captains expect to stay on autopilot during most of the passage up Chesapeake Bay. Some autopilot units change over quickly and simply; some of the more sophisticated systems, however, are harder to operate if you are not familiar with them.

(BH) The reliance on automation, especially autopilots, is excessive.

SHIPBOARD FATIGUE

(GQ) As pilots, we see crew fatigue through the bridge crew, which of course is also often the cargo crew that just finished operations before debarkation.

(BH) Fatigue, as shown by the bridge crew, is chronic. In effect, the master relies entirely on the ability of the pilot.

(JH) Current crew levels create a lot of overtime, for a long period. Reducing the crew numbers only makes that situation worse and makes the crew chronically short handed.

(JB) What are the effects of having fatigued mates making decisions? "It is our strong belief that reductions in manning have had and will have a direct negative effect on vessel operational safety."

HEALTH/DISABILITY

(JH) Reduced manning and a shortage of unlicensed crew members have created health and disability situations that are not tolerable. Unlicensed personnel have been forced to return to work after injuries while officially on restricted or light duty, because of a shortage of personnel in the fleet. The USCG should act on this type of problem, because it compromises the safety of the vessel. The USCG should only allow 100 percent fit-for-duty personnel to serve on these ships.

SHIPBOARD REPAIR CAPABILITY

(DD) Ships' crews are dangerously dependent on the successful operation of the automated equipment. Some operators are removing radio-electronics officers, considering them obsolete, just as other operators are recognizing the increased need for an "onboard maintainer" who can be responsible for the upkeep of the increasing electronics on the vessels.

SHIPBOARD CLEANLINESS

(BH) Smaller crewed ships are dirtier generally, because the crew has too many other things to do and is also expected to do the housework. Riding gangs are used to do routine maintenance on some ships, but these people have no interest in keeping the ship clean. Riding gangs can get away with making a mess in the engine room and leaving it to the crew to clean up after them.

ADEQUATE MAINTENANCE

(JH) Shipboard maintenance suffers with reduced crews, with regular maintenance being postponed or neglected. Poor maintenance endangers the sailors and the vessels.

AUTOMATION RE: SKILL LOSSES

(GQ) The safety problems created by reduced manning are visible principally on foreign-flag vessels, where the crew numbers are now typically 14-18. The reliance on automation is excessive.

(DD) Seafarers are specialists in their trades. Shifting specialized duties to other busy crew members is dangerous, since those crew members will not have the time to learn the necessary skills. An example is the shift of the radio officers' duties to ship captains.

(JH) Able-bodied seaman is not an entry level job, as it is now being treated. It is a journeyman-level unlicensed billet and it has traditionally been attainable by serving time at sea as an ordinary seaman and gaining enough shipboard experience that you could prove to the USCG that you were a skilled AB. It is not appropriate to hire an inexperienced licensed officer to fill a job that should be filled by an experienced unlicensed crew member.

AUTOMATION RE: TRAINING LOSSES

(AT) Some crew reduction schemes eliminate the entry level or second tier ratings for unlicensed billets. Loss of apprentice crew billets has hurt our ability to provide the training and experience needed to competently fill the more senior unlicensed jobs.

AUTOMATION RE: WORK SAVING

(JP) We have also seen that installing automation does not reduce the crew's workload, because that automation does break and you are forced to resort to manual methods, without adequate personnel to carry the load. That burden for physical labor falls heavily on the few remaining unlicensed seamen on the ships.

(JH) The new automation does not reduce workloads, because it does not work as reliably as advertised. What that means is that when you have to go out on deck to take tank readings, you are working on a tanker deck that is laid out all wrong for a crew member to move around the deck easily.

(JB) Is present automation sufficiently reliable, redundant, and user friendly to allow reduced crews on merchant ships? Bridge automation is designed and manufactured by nonmariners who care more for marketing the devices than for the seamen who will have to use them at sea. There is little standardization (for example, among ARPA console configurations), and that makes the job of the mariner much more difficult.

SMALLER CREWS GENERALLY

(GQ) Crews complain about the small numbers and have said that at least 20 people are what they should have on board.

(BH) Smaller crews and the practices that crews are forced to use to deal with working in a smaller crew need to be reversed.

(DD) The problems associated with reduced manning include the high cost of automation and overreliance on its operation, the stress and fatigue suffered by the crew, the loss of necessary specialized crew members' skills, and reduced safety.

(JB) The only practical approach to remove the variable of manning from the international competitive race is to establish an international convention that sets forth minimum *operational* manning, not merely minimum *safe* manning.

(RB) We are convinced that reduced crew size, reduced maintenance and increased exhaustion have reduced the margin of error, and that we run the risk of vastly greater costs if an accident does occur.

SAFETY GENERALLY

(DD) In the interests of protecting maritime safety, we need to have well-maintained ships and well-rested crews.

(AT) Unsafe ships are being safely navigated across the world's oceans every day.

FATIGUE GENERALLY

(JB) The enclosed statements of in-port work routines show how hard mates are pushing themselves and how they are coping with the fast pace of today's cargo operations. We are very concerned about this situation. Nobody can pinpoint the limits of human performance, or pinpoint at what point the hours of work are going to have a deleterious effect on decision making, but this is certainly an area that needs attention.

NEED FOR ACCURATE STATISTICS

(DD) Automation is assumed to reduce work, but the phenomenon of reduced crews is so new that the problems created by working on a reduced crew ship are not adequately recognized. The result is that the agencies accept ship owners' proposals for crew structures even where the agencies cannot account decisively for the consequences of the crew structure changes.

INADEQUATE REGULATORY (COAST GUARD) RESPONSES

RE: ENFORCEMENT

(JH) The USCG must begin to enforce the laws on manning, instead of caving into pressure to allow continued demanning.

(DO) Manning statutes are intended to protect the sailor and need to be enforced as they are written.

(JB) The six-hour rest rule is more often breached than honored.

(RB) Section 8104(d) enforcement of the eight-hour day protection has been distorted. The current interpretation is that "the presence of an overtime rate in a collective bargaining agreement implies that there is no statutory limit to the number of hours a seaman can be required to work in a day."

(JP) The USCG has not been responsive to our concerns. For example, there seems to be no agreed to definition of what exactly a "specially trained ordinary seaman" is, yet it appears on official documents establishing vessel manning.

RE: DECISIONMAKING

(DD) The regulatory agency personnel have inadequate knowledge of the way crews work to carry out their duties.

(AT) Manning decisions must change to consider more than raw numbers.

(DO) The USCG is too heavily influenced by the companies it is intended to regulate. Manning is only one area where this is happening, but it is sad to see the Coast Guard dismissing labor reports of maritime statute violations as a labor-management issue with which they are forbidden to become involved.

(RB) In this atmosphere, relating crew size to the amount of automation on a ship is not justified. The reliance on automation to make these decisions discards the importance of guaranteeing safety through having adequate numbers of qualified crew members on a ship.

(JP) The Coast Guard personnel themselves need better direction than they have been given to date. In general, too many things are being accepted and made apparently permanent, without the authorities being able to evaluate the effects of their own decisions.

CONFLICT OF STATUTE AND PRACTICE

(JH) Unlicensed crew members have taken the brunt of the manning reductions and crew structure changes, such as the maintenance department proposals. We think that the shipping industry should be able to let managers work to efficiently operate without constantly coming at manning levels and aiming at manning.

(DO) The maintenance department concept, which has been proposed by ship owners and accepted by the USCG, has no legal standing in the current statute and should be declared illegal.

(JP) Crew reductions have taken a disproportionate toll on the unlicensed seamen, eliminating their billets or converting them to some sort of maintenance department billet.

ACCURACY OF ECONOMICS, MONETARY SAVINGS

(JB) Are crew cuts cost effective and do they yield any competitive advantage? Any good innovation has been adopted by our competitors and crew reduction is the same situation, so any advantage is temporary.

(TS) The committee must address *why* manning has become such an international squeeze and should examine the economic advantage claims that are made for reducing ship crew numbers. The true international situation is much more extreme than presented here to the committee.

(RB) Foreign sources have conceded that crew reductions will not solve their competitive cost problems, and the flagging out from traditional maritime nations will continue.

COMMITTEE STUDY METHODS

(DD) A truly factual study on reduced manning must examine the work load of crew members and the distribution of the work load, the safety of operations, the shifts of operations and management within the shipping company, the skills and training opportunities for reduced crew seamen, the increased dependence on shoreside maintenance services, and the stress and fatigue that result among the members of a smaller crew.

(DO) The Marine Board should rephrase its question to "Is it possible to ensure the safety of the environment, crew members, vessel, and public interest by use of highly automated smaller crew vessels?"

(TS) International Labor Organization (ILO) resolution 147 went into effect in June 1989. It provides for some port state control authority that the United States could exercise, but the USCG would need some help from the Department of Labor. The committee should examine that newly enacted resolution.

(RB) Seamen work a seven-day week and the committee must examine the actual workload being carried by smaller crews, so that we can really know how labor-intensive our current so-called highly automated fleet is.

(JB) The committee should take the following steps:

1. identify all shipboard tasks under normal operations and emergency operations;
2. identify all legal obligations and correlate them with the shipboard tasks;
3. compare the workload on short versus long voyages, considering the number of port calls and the length of time between each port call;
4. compare the cost of all shipboard automated systems and their required redundancies with the cost of current or future manning levels; and
5. determine the effect that nonstandardization of automated shipboard systems has on learning, operating, reliability, and cost.

Bibliography

The information offered to the committee took several atypical forms: oral remarks, prepared written statements, papers prepared for other meetings, letters, raw data on shipboard work hours, unpublished reports from other organizations, news articles, and personal testimonials. In addition, some remarks emerged during the question and answer periods. A bibliography of this diverse resource material follows.

Don Dishinger, Technical Director, Radio Electronics Officers Union. Mr. Dishinger submitted the following documents before the meeting:

Dishinger, D. M. 1989. Letter to Ms. Lissa A. Martinez (Marine Board), August 21, 1989, with enclosures: California Senate. 1989. Joint Resolution No. 32 Relative to Oil Tanker Accidents.
Dishinger, D. M. and H. Strichartz. 1987. Report on the Twentieth Session of the International Maritime Organization Sub-Committee on Standards of Training and Watchkeeping, January 15, 1987.
Dishinger, D. M. and H. Strichartz. Undated. Report on the International Telecommunications Union 1987 World Administrative Radio Conference in Geneva, Switzerland (undated).

International Maritime Organization. 1987. Subcommittee on Radiocom- munications Document No. COM/34/3/12. Maritime distress and safety system, at-sea, on-board maintenance: An objective study of contem- porary radio electronics officer training. Note by the ICFTU, Novem- ber 18, 1987. London.

International Maritime Organization. 1987. Subcommittee on Radiocom- munications Document No. COM/34/3/13. Maritime distress and safety system, training requirement schedule, a guide to the calculation of time for education in maritime electronics communications and main- tenance technology under GMDSS. Note by the ICFTU, November 19, 1987. London.

International Maritime Organization. 1987. Subcommittee on Standards of Training and Watchkeeping Document No. STW20/2. Decisions of other IMO bodies, Fifty-fourth session of the Maritime Safety Committee. Note by the Secretariat, August 21, 1987. London.

International Maritime Organization. 1987. Subcommittee on Standards of Training and Watchkeeping Document No. STW20/6. Fatigue factor in manning and safety. Note by the ICFTU, November 6, 1987. London.

International Maritime Organization. 1987. Subcommittee on Standards of Training and Watchkeeping Document No. STW20/6/1. Fatigue factor in manning and safety. Note by the United States, November 18, 1987. London.

International Maritime Organization. 1987. Subcommittee on Standards of Training and Watchkeeping Document No. STW20/ Inf. 4 (agenda item 6). Fatigue factor in manning and safety. Practical implications of fatigue. Note by the ICFTU, December 15, 1987. London.

International Maritime Organization. 1987. Subcommittee on Standards of Training and Watchkeeping Document No. STW20/ Inf. 5 (agenda item 6). Fatigue factor in manning and safety. Fatigue and stress, manning and safety on board merchant ships. Note by IFSMA, December 17, 1987. London.

International Maritime Organization. 1988. Maritime Safety Committee. Document No. MSC 55/3/8. Radiocommunications, maritime distress and safety system, verification of performance analysis submitted by India. Note by the ICFTU, February 22, 1988. London.

Dishinger, D. M. 1987. The future global maritime distress and safety system—a trade union response. International Transport Workers Fed- eration, London. 1987.

Mochrie, George. 1988. Future Looks Promising for the Onboard Main- tainer. Safety At Sea, #236, pp. 10-12.

Exxon Shipping Company. 1989. Letter to all masters of Exxon Shipping Company oceangoing vessels. August 7, 1989.

Exxon Shipping Company. 1989. Crew list of *Exxon Jamestown*, October 1962 (indicates 45 men) and August 10, 1989 (indicates 21 men).

Dishinger, D. M. and H. Strichartz. 1989. Manning Reductions and the loss of essential skills. A prepared statement of the Radio Electronics Officers Union for the committee. September 14, 1989.

Mr. Dishinger additionally submitted the following documents after the meeting:

Dishinger, D. M. 1989. Letter, D. Dishinger Radio Electronics Officers Union to W. M. Benkert, Chairman, Committee on the Effect of Smaller Crews on Maritime Safety, September 18, 1989.

Coughlin, W. 1989. Ship cutbacks stir safety fears, page 1. Boston Globe, September 18, 1989.

The Boston Globe. 1989. Forgetting the *Valdez*, editorial, page 18, September 18, 1989.

Coughlin, W. 1989. Teaching plan assailed at radio-exam school for oil-tanker captains, page 12. Boston Globe, September 19, 1989.

Cooperman, A. 1989. Associated Press Radio wire printout. FCC decision to waive radio operator requirement sparks concern (2 p.), September 19, 1989.

Mr. John Hillman, Board of Governors, Exxon Seamen's Union. Mr. Hillman submitted the following documents before the meeting:

Exxon Seamen's Union. 1989. Letter, John L. Hillman Exxon Seamen's Union, to Lissa A. Martinez, Marine Board, July 12, 1989, with enclosures.

Exxon Shipping Company. 1989. Circular letter M-252-02, minimum manning of vessels in port, Exxon shipping company to masters and chief engineers Exxon Shipping company oceangoing vessels, June 26, 1989.

Exxon Shipping Company. 1989. Circular letter Exxon Shipping Company M-250-05, Engineers on watch, to masters and chief engineers of Exxon Shipping Company oceangoing Vessels, May 5, 1989.

Cahill, R. 1985. Chapter IX, Inadequate manning, pages 106 to 109, the case of the VLCC *Esso Cambria*. Strandings and their Causes. London. Fairplay Publications.

Mr. Hillman submitted a prepared statement at the meeting.

Hillman, J.L. 1989. Statement prepared by John L. Hillman to present on September 14, 1989 to the National Research Council's Committee on the Effect of Smaller Crews on Maritime Safety, with enclosures:

National Transportation Safety Board. 1989. Deposition of John Hillman before the National Transportation Safety Board in the matter of the grounding of the tank vessel *Exxon Valdez* near Bligh Island in Prince William Sound near Valdez, Alaska on March 24, 1989 at about 0104. Case No. DCA 89 MM 040. June 1, 1989.

Exxon Shipping Company. 1988. Letter H. J. Borgen, Exxon Shipping Company, to John L. Spencer, Exxon Seamen's Union, regarding WCF grievance #288 not fit for duty status, March 4, 1988.

Exxon Seamen's Union. 1988. Letter John Spencer Exxon Seamen's Union, to H. Borgen, Exxon Shipping Company, February 12, 1988.

Exxon Shipping Company. 1988. Letter D. K. Walker, Exxon Shipping Company to Mr. John Hillman, Exxon Seamen's Union, regarding grievance # 016-88 limited duty, L. Barrett, May 19, 1988.

Exxon Seamen's Union. 1988. Memorandum *Exxon Long Beach*, Exxon Seamen's Union to Board of Governors, Exxon Seamen's Union, regarding urgent USCG investigation, December 18, 1988.

United States Coast Guard. 1989. Vessel file operating details, *Exxon Wilmington*, 12 May 1989.

Mills, T. 1988. Letter Thomas L. Mills, attorney for Exxon Shipping Company (Dyer, Ellis, Joseph and Mills), to Rear Admiral J. W. Kime, Chief, Office of Marine Safety, Security and Environmental Protection, USCG, April 27, 1988.

Mr. Hillman additionally submitted the following documents after the meeting:

Exxon Seamen's Union. 1989. Letter, John Hillman for Exxon Seamen's Union to Charles A. Bookman, Marine Board, September 21, 1989.

Exxon Seamen's Union. Notes Re: February 12, 1988 grievance for unfit for duty AB seaman.

Exxon Shipping Company. 1988. Letter H. J. Borgen, Exxon Shipping Company, to John L. Spencer, Exxon Seamen's Union, regarding WCF grievance #288 not fit for duty status, March 4, 1988.

Exxon Seamen's Union. 1988. Letter John Spencer Exxon Seamen's Union, to H. Borgen, Exxon Shipping Company, February 12, 1988.

Exxon Shipping Company. 1988. Letter D. K. Walker, Exxon Shipping Company to Mr. John Hillman regarding grievance #016-88 limited duty, L. Barrett, May 19, 1988.

Exxon Seamen's Union. Notes Re: April 12, 1988 Exxon Attorney's (T. Mills) letter to Admiral Kime, USCG.

Exxon Seamen's Union. Notes Re: April 27, 1988 Exxon Attorney's (T. Mills) letter to Admiral Kime USCG.

Exxon Seamen's Union. Notes Re: Crew concerns for safety during engine failures on UMS Vessels.

Exxon Seamen's Union. Notes Re: Minimum Manning of vessels in port, eight required (four with licenses and at least two ABs).

Exxon Seamen's Union. Notes Re: two Engineers required on watch.

Exxon Seamen's Union. Notes Re: Exxon Private Memorandum to eliminate QMED overtime on vessels where crew reductions sought.

Exxon Shipping Company. Memorandum. Exxon Private. Subject: 75k DWT class UMS and fleet engine department unlicensed demanning, from S. W. McRobbie. 75K DWT class UMS/Demanning *Exxon Baytown/Exxon Galveston* Demanning.

Exxon Shipping Company. Memorandum. Exxon Private. Subject: UMS/MOA demanning of 75K DWT class 11/3/88, from S. W. McRobbie.

Exxon Seamen's Union. Notes Re: November 3, 1988 Exxon Private Memorandum MOA demanning of 75K.

Exxon Shipping Company. Memorandum. Exxon Private. Subject: QMED Overtime authorized and categorized on UMS Vessels, October 25, 1988.

Exxon Seamen's Union. Notes Re: October 25, 1988 Exxon Private memorandum *Exxon Baytown* QMED overtime.

Exxon Seamen's Union. Notes Re: May 27, 1988 Captain Janecek letter to Paul Meyers deleting three oilers on *Long Beach* and *Valdez.*

United States Coast Guard. 1988. Letter Captain R. A. Janecek, Officer in Charge of Marine Inspection, Los Angeles/Long Beach, to Mr. Paul Meyers, Exxon Shipping Company, subject *Exxon Long Beach, Exxon Valdez,* reduced engine room manning—periodically unattended, May 27, 1988.

Exxon Seamen's Union. Notes Re: January 28, 1988 CDR. Larson letter to Paul Meyers about *Valdez* and *Long Beach* manning.

United States Coast Guard. 1988. Letter CDR Paul T. Larson, Chief Inspection Department, Officer in Charge of Marine Inspection, Los Angeles/Long Beach, to Mr. Paul Meyers, Exxon Shipping Company, subject *Exxon Long Beach, Exxon Valdez,* automation/reduced manning, January 28, 1988.

Exxon Seamen's Union. Notes Re: QMED's deletion, letter May 16, 1989, JLH.

United States Coast Guard. 1989. Letter F. J. Grady, Chief, Merchant Vessel Personnel Division to Mr. John Hillman, Exxon Seamen's Union, May 16, 1989.

United States Coast Guard. 1989. Letter F. J. Grady, Chief, Merchant Vessel Personnel Division to Captain George Wood, Exxon Shipping Company, February 2, 1989

Exxon Shipping Company. 1988. Letter G. N. Wood, Exxon Shipping Company to Capt. F. J. Grady, Chief, Merchant Vessel Personnel, March 14, 1989.

Exxon Shipping Company. 1988. Letter G. N. Wood, Exxon Shipping Company to Capt. F. J. Grady, Chief, Merchant Vessel Personnel, August 22, 1988.

Exxon Shipping Company. 1988. Letter G. N. Wood, Exxon Shipping Company to Capt. F. J. Grady, Chief, Merchant Vessel Personnel, March 17, 1988.

United States Coast Guard. 1989. Letter Capt. F. J. Grady, Chief, Merchant Vessel Personnel, to Mr. Paul B. Meyers Exxon Shipping Company, March 28, 1989.

Exxon Shipping Company. 1989. Letter Mr. Paul B. Meyers, Exxon Shipping Company, to Officer in Charge of Marine Inspection, Portland, Oregon, February 22, 1989.

Exxon Shipping Company. 1989. Memorandum Leonard C. Pittman, Chief Engineer, *Exxon Benicia*, to Paul Meyers, Exxon Shipping Company, February 18, 1989.

United States Coast Guard. 1989. Rapidraft Letter, Officer in Charge of Marine Inspection, Portland, Oregon, to Commandant (G-MVP-4), March 2, 1989.

United States Coast Guard. 1989. Letter F. J. Grady, Chief, Merchant Vessel Personnel Division to Captain George Wood, Exxon Shipping Company, April 25, 1989.

Exxon Seamen's Union. 1989. Minutes, May 1989 Safety Meeting, S/S *Exxon Baton Rouge*, May 3, 1989, signed Emilio Fernandez-Sierra.

George Blumenthal. 1989. Letter to John Hillman, Exxon Seamen's Union, March 10, 1989, regarding a near-miss accident on the *Exxon Valdez*.

Exxon Shipping Company. 1989. Personnel semi-monthly time summary/seagoing, Exxon Shipping Company deck overtime, May 2, 1989.

Exxon Seamen's Union. Notes Re: a QMED on the *Baton Rouge*—JLH.

Exxon Seamen's Union. 1989. Letter John Hillman Exxon Seamen's Union, to USCG official (undesignated), March 7, 1989.

Exxon Shipping Company. 1989. Personnel semi-monthly time summary/seagoing, Exxon Shipping Company, engine overtime, *Exxon Baton Rouge*, for Kenneth A. Farley April 16, 1989, May 2, 1989, May 16, 1989, June 4, 1989.

Exxon Shipping Company. 1989. Personnel semi-monthly time summary/seagoing, Exxon Shipping Company, engine overtime, *Exxon Baytown*, for Alan B. Cash dated December 31, 1988, January 16, 1989, January 19, 1989, and *Exxon Yorktown* for February 16, 1989.

Exxon Shipping Company. 1989. Personnel semi-monthly time summary/seagoing, Exxon Shipping Company, engine overtime, *Exxon Baytown* for Guy C. Picou dated February 1, 1989, February 16, 1989.

Exxon Shipping Company. Personnel semi-monthly time summary/seagoing, Exxon Shipping Company, engine overtime, *Exxon Benicia* for John C. Munich, no date.

Exxon Shipping Company. 1989. Personnel semi-monthly time summary/seagoing, Exxon Shipping Company, engine overtime, *Exxon Philadelphia* for Jeffrey L. Straley dated September 16, 1988, October 5, 1988, October 17, 1988, October 31, 1988, January 18, 1989, February 1, 1989, February 15, 1989.

Exxon Shipping Company. 1989. Overtime report by position code CMS (note: this is a QMED pumpman), Exxon Shipping Company, *Exxon Valdez*, dated February 18, 1989.

Exxon Shipping Company. 1989. Overtime report by position code MOA (note: this is a QMED oiler), Exxon Shipping Company, *Exxon Valdez*, dated February 18, 1989.

Coughlin, W. P. 1989. Exxon managers say company pushes dangerous seagoing policies. Boston Globe, no date.

Letter Frank J. Iarossi, Exxon Shipping Company to John L Hillman, Exxon Seamen's Union, regarding grievance # 034-88 Mandatory Overtime *Exxon Yorktown*, October 14, 1988.

Exxon Shipping Company. Date unknown. Background information for masters mandatory overtime and crossing departmental lines, signed by D. J. Paul, ESC Houston.

DuPont Management Consulting Services. 1988. Excerpt page 3 from a report to Exxon Shipping Company, with notation that report is dated June 1988 (incomplete reference).

Exxon Seamen's Union. 1989. Letter (signature illegible) *Exxon Valdez* at sea, to the governors of the ESU, January 2, 1989 (incomplete reference).

Exxon Seamen's Union. 1989. Notes of phone call from Jesse Kyle, regarding a May 10, 1989 accident on the *Exxon Lexington*, dated September 7, 1989.

Letter Melvyn Drayton, Exxon Shipping Company Personnel Administration Supervisor, to Mr. John Hillman, Esso Seamen's Association, regarding grievance #317 light duty, October 16, 1984.

Exxon Seamen's Union. 1984. Letter John Hillman Esso Seamen's Association, to Melvin Drayton Exxon Shipping Company, regarding grievance #307 sick leave vs. paid leave, Robert Baker, September 19, 1984.

Exxon Shipping Company. 1984. Letter (signature illegible initials SPR) Exxon Shipping Company to Mr. Millard Stanford, Esso Seamen's Association, regarding Grievance #307, sick leave vs. paid leave, Robert Baker, June 25, 1984.

Exxon Seamen's Union. 1984. Letter Robert Knight. Esso Seamen's Association, to Mr. Paul Revere, Exxon Shipping Company, May 21, 1984.

Exxon Seamen's Union. Handwritten notes, unsigned Exxon Seamen's Union. 1988. Letter John Hillman, to Admiral Paul A. Yost, USCG, regarding the Lejano fatality on *M/V Galveston*, March 30, 1988.

Exxon Seamen's Union. 1988. Letter John Hillman, to R. A. Janecek, USCG Marine Safety Office Long Beach, California, March 30, 1988.

Exxon Seamen's Union. 1988. Letter John Hillman, Exxon Seamen's Union, to R. A. Janecek, USCG Marine Safety Office Long Beach, California, March 11, 1988.

United States Coast Guard. Letter R. A. Janecek, Commanding Officer Marine Safety Office, Los Angeles/Long Beach, to John Hillman, Exxon Seamen's Union, with enclosure Report of Marine Accident, Injury, or Death regarding death of Reynaldo Lejano aboard the *Exxon Galveston*, February 2, 1984.

Exxon Seamen's Union. 1988. Letter John Hillman, Federal Freedom of Information Act request to USCG Marine Safety Office Long Beach, California, February 16, 1988.

Exxon Shipping Company. 1984. Letter (signature illegible initials SPR) Exxon Shipping Company, to Mr. John Hillman, Esso Seamen's Association, regarding Damon L. Wenzel fatality, December 13, 1984.

Exxon Shipping Company. Undated. Exxon Shipping Company Safety Credo. Exxon Seamen's Union. 1984. Letter John Hillman, Esso Seamen's Association, to Mr. Paul Revere, Exxon Shipping Company, October 5, 1984.

Exxon Seamen's Union. 1985. Letter John Hillman, Esso Seamen's Association, to Mr. Paul Revere, Exxon Shipping Company, February 21, 1985.

Kopp, Q. 1989. Added staffing on vessels needed to avoid disaster. Half Moon Bay Review, page 5A, Wednesday, July 12, 1989.

Coughlin, W. P. 1989. Exxon ship ignored hurricane gusts to reach *Valdez*, seaman says. The Boston Sunday Globe (page blurred) September 3, 1989.

United States Coast Guard. 1987. USCG 1987 Certificate of Inspection *Exxon Long Beach* (page 1 only), dated April 2, 1987.

Exxon Seamen's Union. 1988. Letter, John Hillman, Exxon Seamen's Union, to Captain F. J. Grady, Chief, Merchant Vessel Personnel, USCG, October 9, 1988.

Exxon Shipping Company. 1989. Letter, J. F. McDermott, Fleet Manning Coordinator, to Mr. Donnie R. Murray re: Attendance counseling, September 25, 1989.

Mr. Augie Tellez, Vice President, Seafarers International Union of North America, AFL-CIO.

Tellez, A. 1989. Statement of the Seafarers International Union of North America, AFL-CIO before the Committee on the Effect of Smaller Crews, September 14, 1989. 8 pages.

Daniel O'Shea, Alliance of Independent Maritime Organizations

O'Shea, D. 1989. A prepared statement of the Alliance of Independent Maritime Organizations. The invasion of the sixty-hour workweek standard and manning reductions in the U.S. maritime industry. Submitted to the Marine Board Committee on The Effects of Smaller Crews on Maritime Safety, September 14, 1989.

Mr. John Bobb, Academic Director of the Maritime Institute of Technology and Graduate Studies, International Organization of Masters, Mates and Pilots.

Bobb, J. 1989. Statement of the International Organization of Masters, Mates and Pilots on Manning, before the Marine Board, September 14, 1989, 29 pages. (Includes 12 signed first-hand duty reports from mates and masters.)

Mr. Richard Berger, Director of Research and Development, Marine Engineers Beneficial Association/National Maritime Union (MEBA 1/NMU) (AFL-CIO).

Berger, R. 1989. Statement by District No. 1—MEBA/NMU before the National Research Council, September 14, 1989, presented on behalf of union president C. E. DeFries.

Mr. Talmadge Simpkins, AFL-CIO Maritime Committee.

Mr. Simpkins provided the following documents after the meeting:

U. S. Congress, House, 1989. A bill to extend the coverage of certain federal labor laws to foreign flag ships, H.R. 3283, 101st Congress, 1st Session. September 18, 1989.

U. S. Department of Labor. 1989. Letter Dennis E. Whitfield, Deputy Secretary of Labor, to Mr. Talmadge E. Simpkins, Executive Director, AFL-CIO Maritime Committee, January 25, 1989.

AFL-CIO Maritime Committee. 1988. Letter Mr. Talmadge E. Simpkins, Executive Director, AFL-CIO Maritime Committee, to Honorable Ann McLaughlin, Secretary of Labor, November 2, 1988.

AFL-CIO Maritime Committee. 1987. Letter Mr. Talmadge E. Simpkins, Executive Director, AFL-CIO Maritime Committee, to Mr. Arthur Rosenfeld, Special Assistant to the Solicitor, U.S. Department of Labor, October 7, 1987.

Attachment A, H.R. 3994, 100th Congress, 2d Session. A bill to extend the coverage of certain federal labor laws to foreign-flag ships, February 24, 1988.

Attachment B, revised language for bill extending coverage of NLRA and FLSA to foreign-flag ships.

Attachment C, memorandum April 11, 1989, extending the National Labor Relations Act and the Fair Labor Standards Act to foreign-flag ships.

U.S. Congress. 1988. Congressional Record, Wednesday, February 24, 1988. Extending our laws to foreign-flag ships, extension of remarks by Hon. William (Bill) Clay of Missouri.

Chairman Benkert also asked those attending to continue to forward materials and information to the committee. Additional material provided to the committee:

International Transport Workers' Federation. 1990. Submission to the Eighth session of the ILO/IMO Joint Committee on Training (JCT8), Geneva, September 17-21.

Statement of C. E. DeFries, President, National Marine Engineers' Beneficial Association before the Subcommittee on Merchant Marine of the Committee on Commerce, Science and Transportation, U.S. Senate on the *Exxon Valdez* oil spill, May 10, 1989.

Meeting guest Bruce Carlton, Director of the Office of Maritime Training and Labor, U.S. Maritime Administration, contributed the following documents:

White, D. 1989. Ship course stresses teamwork on bridge. Journal of Commerce, August 29, 1989

United States Merchant Marine Academy. 1989. Bridge management and teamwork, pilot course, August 21–25, 1989. Department of Continuing Education, United States Merchant Marine Academy and Marine Safety International.

Meeting guest Don Sussman, human factors researcher for the United States Department of Transportation, contributed the following document:

Sussman, E. D. and M. Stearns. 1989. Shipboard crew fatigue, safety and reduced manning draft report: Fatigue. Prepared by: U.S. DOT Transportation Systems Center, prepared for MARAD, August 1989.

Meeting guest Eric Sager, National Transportation Safety Board investigator, contributed the following references after the meeting:

Woodward, D. and P. Nelson. 1974. A user-oriented review of the literature on the effects of sleep loss, work rest schedules, and recovery of performance. Office of Naval Research, U.S. Navy. December 1974. Physiology Report No. ACR-206. Available from National Technical Information Service, Document No. AD-A009-778.

Johnson, L. C. and Philip Naitoh. 1974. The operational consequences of sleep deprivation and sleep deficit, 1974. Scientific and Technical Information Facility, Box 33, College Park, Maryland 20740, USA. Available from National Technical Information Service, Document No. AGARD-AG-193.

Mr. Jim Larsen wrote the Marine Board and contributed the following documents after the meeting:

Larsen, J. 1990. Letter, Jim Larsen to Charles Bookman, Marine Board, January 27, 1990, with enclosures:

Larsen, J. 1990. Letter, Jim Larsen to Florin Dente, January 20, 1990.

Larsen, J. 1988. Letter, Jim Larsen to Florin Dente, June 6, 1988. Larsen, J. 1990?. 12-hour day survey (draft).

Appendix D

Maritime Management Perspectives

In late 1988, the committee decided to conduct its own series of interviews to assess the experience with smaller crews of a range of companies operating ships that trade in the United States. Chairman Benkert, in consultation with the Marine Board staff, identified candidate shipping companies representing a range of trades and vessel types.

Letters requesting an interview were mailed in December 1988, enclosing the questionnaire shown below. In the spring and summer of 1989, a series of personal interviews with senior executive maritime managers were conducted by Chairman Benkert with the assistance of Capt. George Ireland, consultant to the committee.

Questionnaire for Shipping Company Interviews
Committee on the Effect of Smaller Crews on Maritime Safety
December 1988

Attached is a questionnaire for use during interviews of ship owners/operators. Its purpose is two-fold; first as a means to ask the proper questions and not overlook any area, and second, to bring uniformity to the information we are seeking, that is, to validate the information we receive by asking the same questions of more than one operator.

The questionnaire is broken down into five areas; personnel, vessel design and equipment, operations, safety experience with small crews and externalities.

It should be kept in mind that the reason for this study is to assess the effect of smaller crews on maritime safety and therefore the questions should be asked with that objective in mind.

Personnel

Assuming that an oceangoing vessel engaged in international trade having a crew of 9 to 11 persons is to be operated by your company, what personnel standards and/or qualifications would you impose so as to maintain an acceptable level of safety?

Source of personnel?

Special qualifications?
  Dual-license requirement or other cross training
  Pilotage experience/qualification
  Medical; any special physical qualifications

Special training?
  Technical training
  Human relations
  Stress management
  Methods
      Simulators
      Tapes

What conditions of employment might be considered, such as incentives, profit sharing, budget performance, length of service, participation in safety programs, etc?

Who would do the actual employing of shipboard personnel?

Would you utilize a ship management company to perform this role for reduced crews?

Is continuity of shipboard personnel a safety concern?

Vessel Design and Equipment

For an oceangoing ship to be safely operated with a crew of 9 to 11 persons some special features, such as labor-saving devices, would have to be designed into the ship. In your opinion, what are the concepts/features/items you would insist upon having in order for the ship to be operated as safely as one manned by 18 to 21 persons?

Pilot house
Engine room

Control systems, such as steering, propulsion, electrical distribution, safety alarms

Deck/mooring equipment

Internal communications

External communications

Primary lifesaving equipment

Cargo and ballast

Safety systems such as fire extinguishing systems, alarms, etc.

What are your thoughts about a small number of persons being able to cope with emergencies such as a machinery space fire?

How often should safety systems be examined and by whom?

What are your expectations of the role of regulatory persons with regard to these systems?

The Coast Guard has promulgated information regarding technical requirements for automation of vital systems, and also requires approved test procedures be maintained aboard for these systems. In your experience, has this been an adequate way to assure that these systems are kept in proper working order?

What safety systems, if any, should be exclusively redundant aboard ships with a reduced crew? For example, should there be multiple means to alert persons in case of fire or other emergency? Should there be additional/back-up fixed fire extinguishing systems?

Operations

What type of ship would you envision being suitable for such reduced manning?

Tanker

Bulk carrier

Container ship

How would such a ship be assisted from shore, i.e., would special support persons be required at ports/terminals for maintenance, etc.?

What are your thoughts about the role of regulatory bodies such as the Coast Guard or the American Bureau of Shipping with regard to overseeing support activity for such a ship?

What are your thoughts/experience about supplementing the core crew with maintenance teams, mooring teams, etc., from time to time?

What training would you require for crew members manning ships having smaller crews so they could deal with emergencies?

What provisions or precautions would you institute so such crews could deal with special circumstances such as extended operation (long hours), or loss of manpower due to sickness, injury, etc.?

What are your thoughts about length of service aboard such a ship for crew members?

Should the regulatory bodies certify such ships for particular routes, taking into account company support resources, or are such ships capable of being certified for operation anywhere?

Safety Experience

Does your company have records you could share regarding safety experience with oceangoing vessels manned with smaller crews?

Has reduction in crew size had measurable effect on vessel casualties, pollution incidents or personnel injuries? Is fatigue an issue to be dealt with? If so, how has your company addressed this issue?

What, if any, conclusions regarding safety have you drawn from your operating experience with these vessels?

Have you experienced any casualties aboard ships with smaller crews that appear to be related to crew size, qualification or training which would be of value to others to learn about?

Externalities

The concept of operating an oceangoing ship with reduced manning has impacts in several areas, some of which influence safety such as availability of qualified crew members, special insurance requirements, maintenance of a seaworthy vessel, etc.

What organizational changes, if any, has your company implemented in order to maintain safe ships with smaller crews?

How is timely maintenance accomplished aboard ships with smaller crews?

What additional (or fewer) shipboard duties occur as a consequence of manning with smaller crews?

What additional measures, if any, would you like to implement in the future aboard your ships manned with smaller crews to improve safety?

Appendix E
Previous Research on
Shipboard Task Analysis

A number of shipboard task analyses have been conducted in recent years, some developed to identify optimal manning levels (Denny, 1987; Stanwick Corporation, 1971) and some to identify fruitful applications of technology in ships, in addition to optimal manning levels (Larsen, 1988; Liverpool Polytechnic, 1986). All of these analyses used similar methodologies: detailed, bottom-up approaches to cataloging shipboard jobs and times required to complete them, qualified by expert interviews with shipboard and shore-based experts.

The Stanwick Corporation (1971) study was an early effort to determine the manpower and skills required to operate and maintain modern (early 1970s) and advanced (early 1980s) technology cargo vessels. The study identified the skills and numbers of personnel required to operate five different ship types (container, RO/RO, LASH, OBO, and bulk oil carriers) and three different propulsion plants (steam, diesel, and gas turbine). The results showed that upgrading crew skills and cross-utilization of personnel could allow safe, efficient operation of present and future ships, at 50 percent of present manning levels (Table E-1). Stanwick also concluded that many shipboard functions could be performed more efficiently and economically by shoreside personnel.

The Stanwick Corporation (1971) used task lists, operations sequence charts and multiple activity tables, qualified by ships' visits and shipboard interviews to validate their findings. Some empirical data were used in the study, primarily preliminary Navy preventive maintenance system (PMS) data that was used to corroborate some of the engineering task estimates.

TABLE E-1 Recommended Manning for Baseline Ships and Systems

| Type of Ship, Plant and Hotel Services | PRESENT TECHNOLOGY | | ADVANCED TECHNOLOGY |
	Present Skill Levels	Upgraded Skill Levels	Upgraded Skill Levels
Containership, Steam, Full Hotel Services	19	18	14
Containership, Diesel or Gas Turbine, Full Hotel	16	16	14
Containership, Diesel or Gas Turbine, Minimum Hotel	13	13	11
Ro Ro/Lo Lo, Steam, Full Hotel	20	19	15
LASH, Steam, Full Hotel	20	19	15
OBO, Steam, Full Hotel	20 (+5)*	19 (+5)*	15 (+4)*
Bulk Oil Carrier, Steam, Full Hotel Services	20	19	15

* Additional personnel required when performing hold changeover and cleaning underway.

Williams (1983) documented manning requirements for diesel liner vessels built after 1960 which were operated by companies receiving federal operating differential subsidies. Williams used two vessels—the SS *American Lancer* and the MV *Sugar Islander*—as baseline vessels, and performed task analyses using multiple activity charts to determine deck, engine and steward department manning levels. Williams calibrated his engine department findings with preventive maintenance system (PMS) data from the *Sugar Islander*, and adjusted the data upward 33 percent to compensate for lost man-hours (coffee breaks, etc.). In addition to supporting a manning reduction from 26 to 22 men (Table E-2), Williams was also suggesting transferring deck preventive maintenance duties and purser/administrative duties shoreside.

Williams performed task analyses for best case and worst case navigation scenarios (good visibility, open waters versus poor visibility, restricted waters, dense traffic), as well as for mooring, cargo, deck and engine PMS operations. Williams was one of the few studies to analyze and recommend manning levels for emergency situations, recommending an emergency crew of nine, (Table E-3) with an auxiliary stand-by team of six in a central emergency response area. Williams also recommended a realignment of

TABLE E-2 Reduced Manning*

1 Master	
1 Chief Mate	
1 2nd Mate	
1 3rd Mate	
1 Radio Officer	
1 Boatswain	
3 ABs	
2 OSs	11
1 Chief Engineer	
2 Assistant Engineers	
2 QMEDs	
1 Wiper	6
1 Chief Steward	
1 Chief Cook	
1 Cook/Baker	
3 Messmen	
2 Utility Men	8
TOTAL	25

*Additional manning reductions (to 22 people) through smaller
steward's department.

deck and engineering responsibilities within the new organizational framework. However, the Williams results were not validated with empirical
data. Liverpool Polytechnic (1986) used a similar research design to determine manning requirements for the UK fleet of the 1990s. A literature
search, research observation voyages on foreign and domestic (UK) ships,
and interviews with shipping officials were used to produce 16 variations to
conventional manning, thought to be more responsive to needs for the UK
merchant fleet heading into the 1990s. Liverpool also performed a detailed
technology analysis to assess the impact of automation and advanced com-
puting systems on the merchant fleet. Liverpool steered away from specific
crew size estimates or recommendations, and instead concentrated on the
issues thought to be most significant in producing efficient, safe UK ship's
complements (role flexibility and flexibility in trading areas). As with the
Stanwick Corporation and Williams studies, the Liverpool study was also
not validated with empirical data.

Denny (1987) reported on a reappraisal and reorganization of shipboard and shoreside operations at Pacific Gulf Marine (PGM), which was

TABLE E-3 Recommended Emergency Manning*

1 Chief Mate	
1 3d Mate	
3 Seamen (ABs or OSs)	
1 1st Assistant Engineer	
1 QMED	
2 Messmen	
TOTAL	9

*Additional manning recommended of 6 people in central emergency location.

driven by a need for more efficient shipping operations. This cooperative program between the government and PGM used organizational and work assessment techniques—interviews, meetings, questionnaires, organizational analyses, time and motion analyses, daily activity logs, and "day in the life of" sessions—to determine PGMs shipboard and shoreside work planning, work distribution, equipment maintenance, and requisite manning. Denny recommended maintenance of the present ship's complements of 20 personnel, and recommended institution of an onboard maintenance department, development of a shipboard management team, a combined navigation/communications watch (eliminating the need for a radio officer in the future), and institution of participative management techniques for both shoreside and shipboard operations.

Denny reports that trial periods instituting the changes were moderately successful, and Coast Guard approval for the maintenance department concept for PGM ships was secured.

Methodologically, Denny used anecdotal assessments, expert opinion summaries, and a man-hour analysis. However, because of the bridge watch-standing hours commitment, the man-hour analysis result showed an overly large requirement for deck personnel. Work hours per task by labor group were calculated and used to support the manning estimates of 20 people for the existing and proposed new crews. The man-hour analysis supported the current manning, although the work load was distributed differently following the study results. Denny recommended more equally distributed work loads (particularly among deck officers), crew performance feedback, and crew continuity.

Yamanaka and Gaffney (1988) report on experiments conducted by a Japanese joint labor-management-government committee, the Japanese Committee on the Modernization of the Japanese Seafarer's System, which conducted a multiyear experiment varying shipboard manning levels and work designs. Six Japanese companies provided pilot vessels for the basic experiment, and each ship operated under 29 identical experimental conditions, with different manning levels (from 22 to 18). This base experiment ran for 8 months in 1979, and found that horizontal and vertical crew linkages were critical to the success of the new shipboard organization. In addition, the study found that deck and engineering officers would require more training to successfully effect the horizontal linkages.

Yamanaka and Gaffney then report on a series of more comprehensive manning experiments (1979-1986), which encompassed such innovations as horizontal linkages, dual purpose crews (officers and crew), and integration of the third officer responsibilities (deck and engine) into a single watch officer position. These innovations were intended for 16-18 man operations, and the verification experiments conducted with these vessels and organizational designs from 1982-1986 laid the groundwork for the Japanese Pioneer ships with crew of 11, which began operating in 1988. This study used empirically validated task analyses as the foundation for the shipboard organizational redesigns.

In experiments at the Netherlands' TNO Institute of Perception, (Schuffel et al., 1989), bridge manning and a variety of different integrated bridge designs were investigated:

- a single-handed conventional bridge,
- a two-handed conventional bridge, and
- an integrated bridge design, the "Ship 90" bridge ("Bridge 90")

with a one-man watch.

The Ship 90 bridge was configured based on the results of a functional task analysis, which considered how best to allocate bridge planning, monitoring, and ship-handling tasks that involved human and machine use of perceptive, information processing, and motor control processes. Based on these analyses, a one-officer work station was designed for the Ship 90 bridge, and a second work station was provided as a back-up and also to serve as a pilot's work station.

Experiments were conducted using the three bridge designs, with an eye to examining the usefulness and efficiencies for the particular designs and attendant optimal bridge manning levels. The Bridge 9/one-man watch navigational performance (measured by deviation from a centerline course) was found to be superior to the other two bridge designs evaluated; path width remained within safe limits 95 percent of the time, in contrast to the two-handed conventional bridge, which resulted in safe path widths only 50 percent of the time. The single-handed conventional bridge fared less well in the bridge evaluations, with path widths measured within safe limits only 37.5 percent of the time, given identical subjects and conditions. Schuffel concludes that because of the accuracy and care with which navigational information is presented in the integrated bridge design with automated decision aids, navigational performance is superior. More importantly, the studies also indicate that navigation in the Bridge 90 environment with the automated decision aids does not increase the mental load of the navigation task.

This study performed a detailed functional analysis of one subset of shipboard tasks—bridge operations—for advanced bridge designs and their attendant manning levels. Manning issues were one piece of the analysis, and were integrally tied to the bridge designs tested. Schuffel determined that a single-manned, advanced technology bridge was safer and more efficient (as measured by the trackkeeping and mental workload parameters) than either of the other two bridge configurations.

These studies provide a perspective on different approaches to arriving at minimum manning levels. Two cautions, however, are important: (1) much of the previous work was not empirically tested, and (2) many of the studies failed to consider reduced manning scenarios in emergency conditions.

REFERENCES

Denny, M. 1987. Shipboard productivity methods. Vols. 1-3. U.S. Department of Transportation, Maritime Administration, Washington, D.C. February.

Larsen, P. Optimal manning for rational ship operation. Paper 88-P008. Det norske Veritas, Høvik, Norway. February.

Liverpool Polytechnic and Collaborating Colleges. 1986. Technology and manning for safe ship operations. Vols. 1-2. Department of Transport. London. November.

Schuffel, H., J. P. A. Boer, and L. van Breda. 1989. The ship's wheelhouse of the nineties: The navigation performance and mental workload of the officer of the watch. Journal of Navigation 42(1):60-72.

Stanwick Corporation. 1971. Merchant marine shipboard crew skills and disciplines study. U.S. Department of Transportation, U.S. Coast Guard, Office of Merchant Marine Safety, Washington, D.C. Report no. MA-RD-900-7202701. December.

Williams, V. E. 1983. Crew rationalization study: ODS liner vessels. U.S. Department of Transportation, Maritime Administration, Office of Research and Development, Washington D.C. April.

Yamanaka, Keiko, and Michael Gaffney. 1988. Effective manning in the Orient. Report from American President Lines to U.S. Department of Transportation, Maritime Administration, Office of Technology Assessment. Cooperative Agreement No. MA-11727, Report No. MA-RD-770-87052. March 15.

Appendix F
Vessel Manning:
New Applications for Old Statutes

Alex Blanton

The power to prescribe minimum manning levels for merchant vessels is vested in the Coast Guard, which, within the confines of watchstanding, work-hour and work-assignment restrictions imposed by statute, has broad discretion to adjust the manning level according to a vessel's nature, service, and equipment.[1] This paper will first review the statutory language, legislative history, and administrative interpretations and judicial construction of the statutes that circumscribe the Coast Guard's discretion, and will then explore how those statutory standards can best be applied to establish reasonable minimum manning levels for modern merchant vessels.

I. *Background*

The minimum crew "necessary for safe operation" of a vessel is prescribed by the Coast Guard on the vessel's certificate of inspection (COI). 46

The author, a retired Coast Guard officer, is a partner in the Washington, D.C. law firm of Dyer, Ellis, Joseph & Mills. This paper is based in part on an article by the late Clinton J. Maguire, "Laws and Rules of the United States Concerning Vessel Manning," which appeared as an appendix to the 1984 Marine Board Study, Effective Manning of the U.S. Merchant Fleet.

[1] Part F of subtitle II of title 46, United States Code (46 U.S.C. §§ 8101-9308), entitled "Manning of Vessels" and composed of Chapters 81, 83, 85, 87, 89, 91 and 93, provides Congress's mandate with respect to merchant vessel manning. The Coast Guard regulations that interpret and implement these vessel manning statutes are codified in 46 C.F.R. part 15. The Coast Guard provides administrative guidance to its field personnel in the form of the Marine Safety Manual (MSM) and Navigation and Vessel Inspection Circulars (NVICs). Most of the relevant portions of these authorities are reproduced in the attachments.

U.S.C. § 8101(a). Traditionally, the standard crew for an oceangoing vessel has been 26 persons: a licensed master, three mates, three or four licensed engineers, enough sailors to have three per watch, and enough unlicensed engine-room personnel on a steam vessel to have three per watch.[2] The statutes that led the Coast Guard to adopt this traditional manning level fall into three categories: watch-standing requirements, work-assignment restrictions and work-hour limitations.[3] Each category is examined in turn.

A. *Watch-standing Requirements*

The traditional practice of operating vessels through the use of a watch system has been mandated by statute since 1915.[4] The current watch-standing statute, 46 U.S.C. § 8104(d), provides:

> On a merchant vessel of more than 100 gross tons . . . the licensed individuals, sailors, coal passers, firemen, oilers, and water tenders shall be divided, when at sea, into at least 3 watches, and shall be kept on duty successively to perform ordinary work incident to the operation and management of the vessel.

This statute has a significant effect on crew size, because at least three persons must be assigned to any position filled by one of the watch-standing categories. The first two categories of seamen addressed by the statute require some clarification.[5]

The first category, licensed individuals, contains a significant assumption. When this category of seamen was added to the statute in 1938, there were the following classes of licenses: (1) master; (2) chief mate; (3) second and third mate (if in charge of watch); (4) engineer; and (5) pilot. (See former 46 U.S.C. § 228).[6]

---

[2] "Master" is defined in 46 U.S.C. § 10101 as the person in command of a vessel, and "seaman" as a person employed in any capacity aboard a vessel. The definitions in that section, which is in Part G of the Code (Merchant Seamen Protection and Relief), are not directly applicable to Part F (Manning of Vessels), but they are consistent with common usage in the context of vessel manning and will be used in this paper. The term "seaman" should not be confused with "sailor," a term reserved for seamen with deck department duties.

[3] In addition to the statutes discussed below which affect manning levels, 46 U.S.C. § 8301(a) explicitly states in terms and numbers that a vessel must carry certain people. In general, for oceangoing merchant vessels, it requires one licensed master, three licensed mates, and a licensed engineer. Additionally, under Chapter 4 of the International Convention for the Safety of Life at Sea, 1974, a radio officer is required on most vessels.

[4] Watch-standing, when first statutorily mandated in 1915, imposed a two-watch system for sailors and a three-watch system for engineers. The statute was amended in 1936 to cover licensed officers, convert sailors to the three-watch system, and add coal passers.

[5] The remaining persons designated for division into watches are all unlicensed engineers. Unlike licensed individuals and sailors, they are designated with precision; unlicensed persons engaged for engine duties other than coal passer, fireman, oiler, or water tender, are not covered by the statute.

[6] Specific statutes went on to deal with (1) Master of steam or sail (former 46 U.S.C. § 226), (2)

Although the present watch-standing provision purports to require all three general categories of licensed officers (i.e., masters, mates, and engineers) to be divided into three watches, it seems certain that the law did not contemplate forcing the master to stand a watch. The statutory requirement for three mates on the great majority of vessels (46 U.S.C. § 8301(a)(2)) reinforces this assumption.[7]

Given the acknowledged status of a master, when Congress in 1936 declared that "the licensed officers . . . shall . . . be divided into at least 3 watches," it must be seen as having incorporated the unstated qualification of officers whose duties are normally accomplished on a watch.[8] And, in general, Congress must have appreciated that the duties of some seamen traditionally involve watch-standing while those of others, especially food handlers and many supernumeraries (e.g., musicians, bartenders, librarians, and supercargoes), do not.

The second category of watch-standers, sailors, is not defined in the statute. The Coast Guard, however, in its regulations defines "sailors" as "those *members of the deck department* other than licensed officers, whose duties involve the mechanics of conducting the ship on its voyage, such as helmsman (wheelsman), lookout, etc., and which are necessary to the maintenance of a continuous watch" 46 C.F.R. § 15.705(b) (emphasis added). Thus seamen who are not members of the deck department or whose duties do not involve conducting the ship on its voyage are not sailors, and, if not included in one of the other categories, need not be assigned to a watch.

Application of the watch-standing statute has been complicated somewhat by inconsistent judicial interpretations. In 1926, when the Supreme Court decided *O'Hara v. Luckenbach S.S. Company*, 269 U.S. 364 (1926) *reversing* 1 F.2d 923 (9th Cir. 1924), the law required sailors to be divided into two watches, but the vessel at issue was using three watches, not just the two required. There were 13 deck seamen on board, three of whom

---

Chief mate, ocean or coastwise, steam or sail, and second and third mate, ocean or coastwise steam (former 46 U.S.C. § 228), and (3) Engineer of any steam vessel (former 46 U.S.C. § 229). Radio operators were not officers and "registered staff officers" were not recognized by statute.

[7] Of lesser importance, but of some value as a precedent, is the fact that the larger passenger vessels generally carried a second licensed master who was denominated "staff captain" or something similar. This officer was not required or expected to stand a watch simply because his duties lay elsewhere in the management of the ship.

[8] From a converse situation, the real world produces another confirming instance. Although engineers are not divided into classes by statute, as deck officers (including the master as deck officer) are, the Coast Guard has created four grades of license: chief, first assistant, second assistant, and third assistant. When a vessel is required to have four licensed engineers by its certificate of inspection, the chief engineer need not, and in fact does not, stand a watch.

were designated as quartermasters.[9] Each watch included a quartermaster and one able seaman. The remaining seven deck seamen were used for day work only. While the lower courts had been satisfied that the watch requirements of the law were met if qualified personnel were selected for quartermaster and lookout duties, the Supreme Court saw the issue as a matter of "equality" of the watches alone. It decreed that the 13 deck seamen had to be divided into equal watches, presumably 4, 4, 5.[10]

By quoting an earlier court of appeals decision, the Supreme Court silently construed the then extant statutory phrase, "ordinary work incident to the sailing and management of the vessel," as including capability in each watch to meet "all the exigencies of the intended route" and "any exigency that is likely to happen." The Court cited allegations that several marine disasters had been worsened by a shortage of able seamen or by incompetency of lifeboat handlers.

Almost immediately after this decision, and under the same law, came a district court decision, *El Estero*, 14 F.2d 349 (S.D. Tex. 1926), *aff'd sub nom. Southern Pacific Co. v. Hair*, 24 F.2d 94 (5th Cir. 1928). Here, the vessel's COI prescribed four able seamen and two seamen. In addition to the required crew, the ship was carrying other seamen for ship maintenance who were not assigned to watches. The court saw the respondent's position thus: "If the ship can satisfy the local inspectors as to her navigation requirements, she may employ as many additional seamen as she wants, without any of them having the protection of that part of the act providing for their division into watches." Despite the Supreme Court's heavy emphasis on the safety purposes of the statute, the district court saw it as a "protection" to the seamen and directed that all be assigned to watches. More importantly, both the district court and the Fifth Circuit specifically rejected the defendant's argument that the additional seamen were not sailors.

The American Shipper (McCrea v. United States), 3 F. Supp. 184 (S.D.N.Y. 1932, modified on rehearing, 1933), *aff'd sub nom. The American Shipper*, 70 F.2d 632 2d Cir. 1934); *aff'd sub nom. McCrea v. United States*, 294 U.S. 23 (1935), still in the era of the two-watch provision for sailors, supplies some curiosities. The court stated the facts as follows:

> [T]he thirteen seamen on the vessel were not as equally divided into watches as that number permitted. Instead, three seamen were placed on each of three watches, and four men were used for day duty and were not on any watch.

---

[9] Both the Supreme Court and the Court of Appeals referred to the deck seamen as sailors. 269 U.S. at 366; 1 F.2d at 923. Apparently the defendant did not argue, and the courts certainly did not consider, the proposition that the statutory term "sailors" does not automatically include all deck seamen.

[10] Under the principle announced by the Court, the division would have been six-seven had the master chosen to comply only with the two-watch requirement. Indeed, he could have chosen a six-watch system with quartermaster and lookout on each.

> It further appears that three oilers were not placed on any watch, but were assigned to day duty. The firemen and water tenders, however, appear to have been equally divided into three watches.

3 F. Supp. at 185.[11] After stating that *O'Hara v. Luckenbach* required all the sailors of a vessel to be divided into watches as nearly equal to each other as the whole number of sailors will permit, the court concluded, citing the *El Estero* case, that "the additional men should also have been divided into watches." 3 F. Supp. at 185.[12]

In a recent watch-standing case, *District 2, Marine Engineers Benef. Ass'n v. Adams*, 447 F. Supp. 72, 75 (N.D. Ohio 1977), the union asked the court to compel both the vessel's owner and the Coast Guard to enforce the three-watch law with respect to the licensed engineers.[13] The court, stating that the "shall enforce" language in the predecessor to 46 U.S.C. § 2103 created a clear, ministerial, and nondiscretionary duty, issued a preliminary injunction requiring the Coast Guard to assess the statutory penalty for violating the three-watch statute. The court concluded that "there exists no authority whatsoever for nullifying the three-watch requirement of [section 8104(d)]." 447 F. Supp. at 81 (emphasis deleted). "While Congress presumably could have left to the Coast Guard the decision as to the system of watches required for the safety of each individual vessel and its crew, it chose instead to prescribe a uniform three-watch requirement for all vessels." *Id.* at 80.[14]

The decisions in all of the foregoing cases share a common defect. The courts apparently did not consider the possibility that the law attached only to seamen whose work was normally performed on a watch-standing basis. Moreover, no thought was given to the basic reality that it is the master who is ultimately responsible for setting watches and not the Coast Guard, which is authorized only to set the complement required.

---

[11]Apparently, since more than 13 seamen are enumerated, the court should have used the term "sailors" instead of "seamen."

[12]Even though the petitioner was a fireman, and the firemen were divided into equal watches, the court allowed him the statutory remedy. The statute then provided: "Whenever the master of any vessel shall fail to comply with this section . . . the seamen shall be entitled to discharge from such vessel." The petitioner was a "seamen" entitled to the remedy. Thus the mates, the licensed engineers, and the cooks are all entitled to discharge if there is a breach.

[13]The COIs at issue required three licensed engineers, one chief and two unclassified assistants, who, apparently with Coast Guard approval, were not assigned to watches. The vessels were equipped with full pilot-house control of the engines, and the engine room was unattended. The three licensed engineers were the only personnel in the engine department.

[14]The value of this case as precedent is questionable. After the preliminary injunction was issued, the dispute was settled and the union dismissed its complaint. Reportedly the union agreed that the licensed engineers would not be required to stand watches in return for a promise by the shipowner not to reduce their number below three.

In contrast to the foregoing cases, *The Chilbar*, 10 F. Supp. 926 (E.D. Pa. 1935) and *The Youngstown*, 110 F.2d 968 (5th Cir. 1940), *cert. denied*, 311 U.S. 690 (1940), present a more functional view of the watch-standing provisions. *The Chilbar* case held that "repairmen" hired and described as part of a "maintenance department" (a term not found in law or regulation) need not be divided into watches. In *The Youngstown*, the court held that a wiper and a boatswain, two positions not mentioned in the statute, were not required to stand watches. "The statute does not require any watches at all for the boatswain and the wiper, and no duty can be violated where none is owed." 110 F.2d at 969.[15] The conflict between these cases and those discussed above is obvious, but no court has ever mentioned it, and some courts cite cases from both groups as if in harmony.

B. *Work Assignment Restrictions.*

Section 8104(e)(1) of Title 46, U.S.C., provides that a seaman may not be (A) engaged to work alternately in the deck and engine departments; or (B) required to work in the engine department if engaged for deck department duty or required to work in the deck department if engaged for engine department duty. Both the Coast Guard and the courts have given this provision a straightforward interpretation. *Smith v. Reinauer Oil Transp.*, 256 F.2d 646, 652 (1st Cir.) (engine room crewmember is permitted, but cannot be required, to work in deck department), *cert. denied*, 358 U.S. 889 (1958); *Kane v. American Tankers Corp.*, 219 F.2d 637, 639 (2d Cir. 1955).

C. *The Work-hour Limitation.*

Under 46 U.S.C. § 8104(d), a "licensed individual or seaman in the deck or engine department may not be required to work more than 8 hours in one day." *See also* 46 C.F.R. § 15.710. A crew member may volunteer for overtime under circumstances lacking "direct or indirect coercion." 3 MSM § 22.C.[16] If, in a collective bargaining agreement or other

---

[15]*Cf. Western Pioneer, Inc. v. United States Coast Guard*, 709 F.2d 1331, 1336 (9th Cir. 1983) (the Coast Guard's strict interpretation of section 8104(d) is entitled to deference). In *The Youngstown* case, the court also addressed the position of an oiler performing the duties of deck engineer, a rating classified as "a qualified member of the engine department" and not enumerated in the three-watch provision. Although the other oilers on board stood watches, the one acting as deck engineer was held not to be subject to the provision on watch division. Apparently, the vessel did not carry a "regular" deck engineer. The seaman in question was apparently signed on precisely as an oiler, and the court, despite that designation, looked at the kind of work he did to determine whether he was subject to the three-watch law.

[16]Note, however, that MSM 22.C instructs the cognizant Coast Guard officers to study carefully any pattern of overtime that might indicate that the vessel is undermanned, with a view toward amending the vessel's COI to require additional crew members.

contract of employment, the crewman (or the union on his behalf) agrees to specific overtime standards, work performed within those standards would be deemed voluntary. *The Youngstown*, 110 F.2d at 970. The owner or master may require a seaman to agree to work a certain amount of overtime as a condition of a seaman's employment. Even then, however, the seaman may unilaterally refuse to work overtime. If that happens, the owner/master may not force the seaman to work overtime during the current period of employment but may refuse to rehire the seaman. *See* paragraph 9 of the attached October 14, 1988 letter from the Chief of the Coast Guard's Merchant Vessel Personnel Division.

Watch duty is considered as time "on duty" included in the eight-hour limit, but in-port night watch-standers are presumed to have voluntarily assumed the additional duty. 3 MSM § 22.D.[17] Although watch duty is included in the calculation of the eight-hour day, a seaman may be required to perform routine maintenance duties while on watch. "The performance of such regular and customary duties, even though of a nature to require the breaking of a watch, was not violative of the statute." *The Youngstown*, 110 F.2d at 969; *see also Southern Pacific Co.*, 24 F.2d at 95 ("[T]here is no requirement that all sailors while on watch be engaged exclusively in [watch-standing-type] work, and that none of them, when his services are not needed for the proper performance of that work, may not be assigned to such work as cleaning, painting, etc.").

II. *Recent Developments: Maintenancepersons and Maintenance Departments.*

Despite the overly restrictive interpretation that courts have tended to give the watch-standing provisions, the existing regime provides some flexibility for adapting manning levels to evolving technological and economic realities. The Coast Guard's manning regulations and other guidelines clearly embrace the concept of a shipboard organization in which not all personnel listed on the COI are required to stand watches. According to 46 C.F.R. § 15.705:

> The Coast Guard interprets the term 'watch' to be the direct performance of vessel operations, whether deck or engine, where such operations would routinely be controlled and performed in a scheduled and fixed rotation. The performance of maintenance or work necessary to the vessel's safe operation on a daily basis does not in itself constitute the establishment of a watch. The minimal safe manning levels specified in a vessel's certificate of inspection take into consideration routine maintenance requirements and ability of the crew

---

[17]But note 46 U.S.C. § 8104(a), under which an officer may "take charge of the deck watch on a vessel when leaving or immediately after leaving port only if the officer has been off duty for at least 6 hours within the 12 hours immediately before the time of leaving."

to perform all operational evolutions, including emergencies, as well as those functions which may be assigned to persons in watches.

The above language, considered in light of the *Chilbar* and *Youngstown* cases discussed above, provides a strong basis for the exemption of maintenance personnel from watch requirements, especially if they are assigned to a separate maintenance department. The key to section 15.705 is its explanation that some of the personnel specified by the COI are needed to perform routine maintenance, while other personnel are needed to perform vessel operations. Personnel performing routine maintenance are not subject to watch-standing requirements, whereas personnel performing vessel operations are. *See also* 3 MSM § 22.E. In short, not every individual specified by the COI must be assigned to a watch. This is not a new position for the Coast Guard. The previous version of the manning regulations (former 46 C.F.R. § 157.20-5(a)) provided, "The requirement for division into watches applies only to those classes of the crew specifically named in [section 8104(d)]."

In a letter to all field Merchant Marine Safety Offices (attached), the Chief of the Coast Guard's Merchant Vessel Personnel Division further supports this interpretation of the statute and regulations. The letter reiterates guidance in the MSM (3 MSM § 22.B) that all personnel in the unlicensed ratings of able seaman, ordinary seaman, fireman-watertender, and oiler, when required by a vessel's COI, are considered watch-standing categories for purposes of 46 U.S.C. § 8104 and must be divided into successive watches and employed for the performance of ordinary work incident to the operation of the vessel. The letter goes on, however, to recognize:

During the past decade, various labor saving devices and operational innovations have enabled navigational watches to be safely and effectively performed with fewer individuals. . . . The recently published [revised] manning regulations recognize that the individual in command of a vessel has knowledge of all of the circumstances necessary to make a decision on the proper composition and conduct of the navigational and machinery space watches. Therefore 46 C.F.R. 15.705(b) specifies that a vessel's master is responsible for the establishment of adequate watches.

In an enclosure entitled "Maintenancepersons," the letter provides extensive guidance on the establishment of a maintenance department aboard vessels:

[S]ome of the individuals in a vessel's Coast Guard mandated crew complement may be engaged as maintenancepersons and assigned to a maintenance department. If properly qualified, these maintenancepersons can be used by the vessel's master to augment navigational or machinery space watches should circumstances such as weather, mechanical failure, etc., require watch augmentation. During periods in which these maintenancepersons are used to augment navigational or machinery space watches, they become part of the watch and are subject to requirements such as the three watch requirement of 46 CFR 15.705.

Once a maintenance department is established, all personnel not required by the vessel's COI can be engaged as maintenancepersons, assigned to the maintenance department, and relieved from watch duty. Engine maintenancepersons required by the COI can be assigned to the maintenance department and relieved from watch duty.[18] With approval of the Coast Guard, three of the six ABs normally required by the COI can be converted to maintenancepersons, assigned to the maintenance department and relieved from watch duty.

Even without amending a vessel's COI to include a maintenance department, it should be possible to designate crew members not required by the COI as maintenancepersons and exempt them, along with crew members identified as maintenancepersons on the COI, from watch duty. If a separate maintenance department is not established, however, such maintenancepersons would necessarily retain their affiliation with either the deck or engine department, and the work assignment restrictions caused by such affiliation, discussed above, would continue to apply.

Once a maintenance department has been established, the law leaves ample room for flexibility in making work assignments for its members. Under 3 MSM § 21.C, "maintenancepersons may be identified by departmental affiliation (deck maintenanceperson, engine maintenanceperson) or by no affiliation, in which case the master has the discretion to determine how to best utilize the person." Based on this language, the shipowner can retain flexibility by making clear that maintenancepersons are not affiliated with either the engine department or the deck department and that they are thus free to alternate between engine and deck duties.

Literally, the eight-hour limitation in 46 U.S.C. § 8104(d) does not apply to persons (licensed or unlicensed) assigned to a maintenance department, and would not affect the ability to require maintenancepersons to work overtime. Unlike the situation with regard to watch-standing and work-assignment restrictions, however, the Coast Guard's regulations and administrative guidance do not support such a literal interpretation regarding the work-hour restriction. *See,* e.g., 3 MSM 22.C ("Seamen [without limitation] may not be required to work more than 8 hours . . . ."); 46 C.F.R. § 15.710 (citing the statute as "set[ting] limitations on the working hours of . . . crew members"). Nonetheless, since the statutory work-hour restriction contains the same restrictive language ("in the deck or engine department") as the other restrictions, it is possible to extrapolate the same

---

[18] The regulations do not explicitly support this rationale for excluding engine maintenancepersons from watchstanding, but it is a logical extension of the rationale used with regard to deck personnel. Without further approval from Coast Guard Headquarters, Qualified Members of the Engine Department (QMEDs) required by the vessel's COI cannot be assigned to the maintenance department. Compare 3 MSM 21.B, authorizing the substitution of "junior engineers, deck engine mechanics, or enginemen" for oilers, but requiring such substitutes to stand watches.

result, namely, that the work-hour restriction does not apply to members of the maintenance department.

Although clearly supportable from a legal (and perhaps, logical) point of view, any attempt to use this rationale for purposes beyond those to which the Coast Guard has been willing to apply it clearly puts the entire maintenance department concept at risk.[19] First, in any court challenge, the position of a regulated party is not accorded the presumption of regularity accorded to the position of a regulatory agency. Second, such an attempt to extend the rationale would undoubtedly cause pressure on the Coast Guard to retrench from other positions based on that rationale. Thus the shipowner should carefully weigh the advantage to be gained from a conclusion that the eight-hour workday limitation does not apply to members of the maintenance department (i.e., the ability to require those crewmembers to work overtime) against the risk that asserting that position would endanger the entire maintenance department concept.

If a maintenance department is established, its actual administration must be consistent with the premise on which it is based—that the ship can be properly maintained and operated by fewer personnel if some of the assigned seamen are dedicated to daywork maintenance. Two practices, in particular, would cast doubt on the validity of that premise. First, frequent use of maintenance department personnel to perform nonmaintenance duties concerning ship operations would indicate that there are not enough seamen assigned to watches. Second, requiring maintenance department personnel routinely to work overtime would indicate that the manning level—regardless of departmental organization—is insufficient for performing routine maintenance. And, of course, combining these two practices—frequent assignment to nonmaintenance duties of a maintenanceperson who is routinely required to work overtime—would be altogether inconsistent with the statutory work-hour restrictions. *Cf.* MSM § 22.C; 23.A.5.

III. *Continuing Problems.*

The current statutory and regulatory regime for vessel manning suffers from several deficiencies that cannot be overcome by administrative innovations. They are at once both too broad and too rigid. The manning code, despite the 1983 recodification, is mostly a conglomeration of disjointed legislative responses to spasmatic maritime disturbances throughout this century. It provides no overall objective that the Coast Guard is expected

---

[19] The primary basis for the eight-hour restriction appears to be the avoidance of fatigue among personnel involved with navigating the vessel and operating its safety systems. Since maintenancepersons are not routinely involved in such activities, logically, they should not be included within the restriction's compass.

to pursue in administering the statutes. On the other hand, the individual provisions tend to focus too narrowly on discrete facets of the manning picture. Their rigidity deprives shipowners, masters, and seamen of the flexibility needed to develop a prosperous merchant fleet.[20]

In 46 U.S.C. § 2103, Congress has directed the Coast Guard to enforce, carry out, and uniformly administer all the shipping statutes for which it is responsible "in the interests of marine safety, and seamen's welfare." This broad statement provides little practical guidance for administering the manning laws. In particular, it fails to inform the Coast Guard and the public how the two stated objectives, marine safety and seamen's welfare, relate to each other or to other factors that affect vessel manning. For example, economic competitiveness—both within the maritime sphere and with other modes of transportation—is obviously a major factor driving the shipowner's desire to decrease crew size. It is also a necessary element in developing and maintaining the type of merchant marine fleet and infrastructure envisioned by section 101 of the Merchant Marine Act, 1936 (46 U.S.C. app. § 1101) (set forth in the attached list of authorities). Another relevant factor, repeatedly highlighted by the Maritime Administration and the Department of Defense, is the need to maintain a pool of qualified merchant mariners for national emergencies. How should these and other factors affect the vessel manning calculus?

The absence of clearly stated policy objectives is a major shortcoming, but it does not present as serious an obstacle to rational treatment of vessel manning issues as does the rigidity of the current watch-standing, work-hour and work-assignment restrictions.

Individually, these provisions may have been rational reactions to the circumstances that gave rise to their enactment.[21] Collectively, however, they needlessly deprive the Coast Guard and the industry of the flexibility

---

[20] As this is being written, it appears that Congress is about to impose yet another disjointed manning restriction in response to a marine disaster. The House of Representatives' version of the Oil Spill legislation that is scheduled to go to conference in January 1990 would add a new subsection (n) to 46 U.S.C. § 8104:

> On a tank vessel, a licensed individual or seaman may not be permitted to work more than 15 hours in any 24-hour period, or more than 36 hours in any 72-hour period, except in an emergency or a drill. In this subsection, "work" includes any administrative duties associated with the vessel whether performed on board the vessel or ashore.

H.R. 1465 § 4117(b), 101st Cong., 1st Sess. (passed by the House on November 9, 1989). While this new work-hour restriction may be entirely reasonable, it would make more sense as part of comprehensive regulations issued by the Coast Guard after public study and rulemaking.

[21] This may be a charitable statement. Neither the work-assignment nor the work-hour restriction, for example, does much to serve either seamen's welfare or marine safety. At best, they provide a crude means of dealing with the issues of strain, fatigue, and boredom.

needed to address the manning issues facing the merchant fleet. The current statutes may not present inordinate obstacles to setting the manning level on vessels whose machinery, equipment, and layout conform to the traditional design, but for newer vessels, designed specifically to minimize personnel requirements, they are awkward at best. More importantly, they inhibit innovation and experimentation.

The problem with the present statutory regime is not so much that it dictates unnecessarily large crews. It does not. The problem is that it deprives the maritime industry of the flexibility needed to best utilize the crew members assigned. Theoretically, current law would allow an oceangoing vessel to operate with as few as five seamen—a master, a licensed engineer and three licensed mates. As a practical matter, however, the Coast Guard is unlikely to approve so small a crew as satisfying the safe operation requirement of 46 U.S.C. § 8101(a). The watch-standing, work-hour, and work-assignment restrictions tend to require increases above that minimum to be supplied in quantums of three (either engineers or deck). As a result, the practical minimum manning under current law is approximately 17—a master, three licensed mates, four licensed engineers, six unlicensed deck seamen and three unlicensed engineers. Again, the problem with this number is not that it represents an unreasonable floor. Most vessels will in fact require more people for safe operation. The problem with the number is that it is derived by using arbitrary parameters that serve no useful purpose in determining how a given vessel should be manned.[22]

In other modes of transportation, where Congress and the public have demonstrated a serious interest, manning issues are regulated in a more sensible manner. In aviation, for instance, Congress has provided broad statutory guidance authorizing the administrator to develop and issue regulations.[23] Under these statutes, the Federal Aviation Authority has issued detailed regulations governing various aspects of aircraft manning.

---

[22]The current statutes also fail to reflect modern concepts of labor-management relations and collective bargaining. They perpetuate the archaic view of seamen as helpless waifs who must be protected not only from the selfish vagaries of masters and owners but also from their own ignorance and intemperance. Such anachronisms hardly provide a basis for a rational approach to manning policy.

[23]The applicable statute is 49 U.S.C. § 1421, which, in relevant part, provides:

(a) Minimum standards; rules and regulations. The [Secretary of Transportation] is empowered and it shall be his duty to promote safety of flight of civil aircraft in air commerce by prescribing and revising from time to time:

(5) Reasonable rules and regulations governing, in the interest of safety, the maximum hours or periods of service of airmen, and other employees, of air carriers; and

(6) Such reasonable rules and regulations, or minimum standards, governing other practices, methods, and procedure, as the [Secretary] may

For example, 14 C.F.R. part 121, subpart M prescribes minimum manning requirements in terms of numbers, and 14 C.F.R. part 135, subpart F prescribes detailed work-hour limitations, for various types of aircraft and operating conditions.[24]

To some extent, this approach transfers the political heat for establishing manning policy from the Congress to the administrative agency. Any statute that bestows the flexibility needed to react to changing conditions necessarily increases the extent to which the administrator must deal with political considerations. And the Coast Guard, which has always been uncomfortable with the political aspects of its regulatory role, may resist a change that will increase its political role. In the end, however, there can be no doubt that the maritime industry would be well served by removing the current artificial impediments and giving the Coast Guard the discretion and flexibility needed to adopt more functional and rational vessel manning regulations.

CONCLUSION

The Coast Guard, by insisting on a pragmatic interpretation, has managed to extract some degree of reason from the present statutes. At the frontiers of manning practices, however, the Coast Guard's position is precarious. Both the Coast Guard and the industry—shipowners, masters, unions and individual seamen—need and deserve a more stable platform on which to construct the manning practices that will take this nation into the twenty-first century.

---

find necessary to provide adequately for national security and safety in air commerce.

(b) Consideration of needs of service; classification of standards, rules, regulations, and certificates. In prescribing standards, rules, and regulations, and in issuing certificates . . ., the [Secretary] shall give full consideration to the duty resting upon air carriers to perform their services with the highest possible degree of safety in the public interest and to any differences between air transportation and other air commerce; and he shall make classifications of such standards, rules, regulations, and certificates appropriate to the differences between air transportation and other air commerce. . . . The [Secretary] shall exercise and perform his powers and duties . . . in such manner as will best tend to reduce or eliminate the possibility of, or recurrence of, accidents in air transportation, but shall not deem himself required to give preference to either air transportation or other air commerce in the administration and enforcement of this title.

[24]The approach to manning in the railroad industry is similar. As with aviation, Congress has given the administrator broad authority to develop, issue and enforce regulations on manning practices. *See* 45 U.S.C. § 431 concerning promulgation of regulations "for all areas of railroad safety." In addition, however, Congress has, by statute, prescribed detailed work-hours restrictions for railroad employees. 45 U.S.C. §§ 61-66; *see also* Federal Railroad Administration regulations at 49 C.F.R. part 228.

LAWS AND RULES CONCERNING VESSEL MANNING

Part I: STATUTES

46 U.S.C. § 2103 Superintendence of the Merchant Marine

> . . . . In the interests of marine safety and seamen's welfare, the Secretary [of the Department in which the Coast Guard is operating] shall enforce and shall carry out correctly and uniformly administer [46 U.S.C §§ 2101-14701].

46 U.S.C. § 8101 Complement of Inspected Vessels

> (a) The certificate of inspection issued to a vessel . . . shall state the complement of licensed individuals and crew (including lifeboatmen) considered by the Secretary to be necessary for safe operation. A manning requriement imposed on—

> > (3) a tank vessel shall consider the navigation, cargo handling, and maintenance functions of that vessel for protection of life, property, and the environment.

> (b) The Secretary may modify the complement, by endorsement on the certificate, for reasons of changed conditions or employment.

> (d) A vessel to which this section applies may not be operated without having in its service the complement required in the certificate of inspection.

46 U.S.C. § 8102 Watchmen

> (a) The owner, charterer, or managing operator of a vessel carrying passengers during the nighttime shall keep a suitable number of watchmen in the vicinity of the cabins or staterooms and on each deck to guard against and give alarm in case of a fire or other danger.

46 U.S.C. § 8104 Watches

> (a) An owner, charterer, managing operator, master, individual in charge, or other person having authority may permit an officer to take charge of the deck watch on a vessel when leaving or immediately after leaving port only if the officer has been off duty for at least 6 hours within the 12 hours immediately before the time of leaving.

> (d) . . . [T]he licensed individuals, sailors, coal passers, firemen,

oilers, and water tenders shall be divided, when at sea, into at least 3 watches, and shall be kept on duty successively to perform ordinary work incident to the operation and management of the vessel. . . . A licensed individual or seaman in the deck or engine department may not be required to work more than 8 hours in one day.

(1) a seaman may not be—

(A) engaged to work alternately in the deck and engine departments; or

(B) required to work in the engine department if engaged for deck department duty or required to work in the deck department if engaged for engine department duty.

(2) a seaman may not be required to do unnecessary work on Sundays, New Year's Day, July 4th, Labor Day, Thanksgiving Day, or Christmas Day, when the vessel is in a safe harbor, but this clause does not prevent dispatch of a vessel on a voyage; and

(3) when the vessel is in a safe harbor, 8 hours (including anchor watch) is a day's work.

(f) Subsections (d) and (e) of this section do not limit the authority of the master or other officer or the obedience of seamen when, in the judgment of the master or other officer, any part of the crew is needed for—

(1) maneuvering, shifting the berth of, mooring, or un-mooring, the vessel;

(2) performing work necessary for the safety of the vessel, or the vessel's passengers, crew, or cargo;

(3) saving life on board of another vessel in jeopardy; or

(4) performing fire, lifeboat, or other drills in port or at sea.

(n) On a tanker, a licensed individual or seaman may not be permitted to work more than 15 hours in any 24-hour period, or more than 36 hours in any 72-hour period, except in an emergency or a drill. In this subsection, 'work' includes any administrative duties associated with the vessel whether performed on board the vessel or onshore.

46 U.S.C. § 8301 Minimum Number of Licensed Individuals

(a) [A] vessel subject to inspection . . . shall engage a minimum of licensed individuals as follows:

(1) Each of those vessels propelled by machinery or carrying passengers shall have a licensed master.

(2) A vessel of at least 1,000 gross tons and propelled by machinery shall have 3 licensed mates. However, if the vessel is on a voyage of less than 400 miles from port of departure to port of final destination, it shall have 2 licensed mates.

(5) A freight vessel or a passenger vessel of at least 300 gross tons and propelled by machinery shall have a licensed engineer.

(d) The Secretary may—

(2) increase the number of licensed individuals on a vessel . . . if, in the Secretary's judgment, the vessel is not sufficiently manned for safe operation.

46 U.S.C. § 8304 Implementing the Officers' Competency Certificates Convention, 1936

(c) A person may not engage or employ an individual to serve as, and an individual may not serve as, a master, mate, or engineer on a vessel . . . if the individual does not have a license issued under section 7101 of this title authorizing service in the capacity on which the individual is to be engaged or employed.

(e) A license issued to an individual to whom this section applies is a certificate of competency.

(f) A designated official may detain a vessel . . . (by written order served on the owner, charterer, managing operator, agent, master, or individual in charge of the vessel) when there is reason to believe that the vessel is about to proceed from a port of the United States to the high seas in violation of this section or a provision of the [Officers' Competency Certificates Convention, 1936]. The vessel may be detained until the vessel complies with this section. Clearance may not be granted to a vessel ordered detained under this section.

(g) A foreign vessel to which the convention . . . applies, on the navigable waters of the United States, is subject to detention under subsection (f) of this section, and to an examination that may be necessary to decide if there is compliance with the convention.

46 U.S.C. § 8702 Certain Crew Requirements

(b) A vessel may operate only if at least—

(1) 75 percent of the crew in each department on board is able to understand any order spoken by the officers, and

(2) 65 percent of the deck crew (excluding licensed individuals) have merchant mariners' documents endorsed for a rating of at least able seaman, except that this percentage may be reduced to 50 percent on a vessel permitted under section 8104 of this title to maintain a 2-watch system.

(d) An individual having a rating of less than able seaman may not be permitted at the wheel in ports, harbors, and other waters subject to congested vessel traffic, or under conditions of reduced visibility, adverse weather, or other hazardous circumstances.

46 U.S.C. § 8703 Tankermen on Tank Vessels

(a) A vessel of the United States to which chapter 37 of this title applies, that has on board oil or hazardous material in bulk as cargo or cargo residue, shall have a specified number of crew certified as tankermen as required by the Secretary. This requirement shall be noted on the certificate of inspection issued to the vessel.

46 U.S.C. § 9101 [Manning] Standards for Foreign Tank Vessels

(a) (1) The Secretary shall evaluate the manning, training, qualification, and watchkeeping standards of a foreign country that issues documentation for any vessel to which chapter 37 of this title applies—

(A) on a periodic basis; and

(B) when the vessel is involved in a marine casualty required to be reported under section 6101(a)(4) or (5) of this title.

(2) After each evaluation made under paragraph (1) of this subsection, the Secretary shall determine whether—

(A) the foreign country has standards for licensing and

certification of seamen that are at least equivalent to United States law or international standards accepted by the United States; and

(B) those standards are being enforced.

(3) If the Secretary determines under this subsection that a country has failed to maintain or enforce standards at least equivalent to United States law or international standards accepted by the United States, the Secretary shall prohibit vessels issued documentation by that country from entering the United States until the Secretary determines those standards have been established and are being enforced.

(4) The Secretary may allow provisional entry of a vessel prohibited from entering the United States under paragraph (3) of this subsection if—

(A) the owner or operator of the vessel establishes, to the satisfaction of the Secretary, that the vessel is not unsafe or a threat to the marine environment; or

(B) the entry is necessary for the safety of the vessel or individuals on the vessel.

(b) A foreign vessel to which chapter 37 of this title applies that has on board oil or hazardous material in bulk as cargo or cargo residue shall have a specified number of personnel certified as tankerman or equivalent, as required by the Secretary, when the vessel transfers oil or hazardous material in a port or place subject to the jurisdiction of the United States. The requirement of this subsection shall be noted in applicable terminal operating procedures. A transfer operation may take place only if the crewmember in charge is capable of clearly understanding instructions in English.

46 U.S.C. § 9102 [Manning] Standards for Tank Vessels of the United States

(a) The Secretary shall prescribe standards for the manning of each vessel of the United States to which chapter 37 of this title applies, related to the duties, qualifications, and training of the officers and crew of the vessel . . .

46 U.S.C. app. § 1101 Merchant Marine Act, 1936; Declaration of Policy

It is necessary for the national defense and development of its foreign and domestic commerce that the United States shall have a merchant marine (a) sufficient to carry its domestic water-borne commerce and a substantial portion of the water-borne export and import foreign commerce of the United States and to provide shipping service essential for maintaining the flow of such domestic and foreign water-borne commerce at all times, (b) capable of serving as a naval and military auxiliary in time of war or national emergency, (c) owned and operated under the United States flag by citizens of the United States, insofar as may be practicable, (d) composed of the best-equipped, and most suitable types of vessels, constructed in the United States and manned with a trained and efficient citizen personnel, and (e) supplemented by efficient facilities for shipbuilding and ship repair. It is hereby declared to be the policy of the United States to foster the development and encourage the maintenance of such a merchant marine.

Part II: RULES

46 C.F.R. § 15.103

(b) The navigation and shipping laws state that a vessel may not be operated unless certain manning requirements are met. In addition to establishing a minimum of licensed individuals and members of the crew to be carried on board certain vessels, they establish minimum qualifications concerning licenses, citizenship, and conditions of employment. It is the responsibility of the owner, charterer, managing operator, master or person in charge or command of the vessel to ensure that appropriate personnel are carried to meet the requirements of the applicable navigation and shipping laws and regulations.

(c) Inspected vessels are issued a certificate of inspection which indicates the minimum complement of licensed individuals and crew (including lifeboatmen) considered necessary for safe operation. The certificate of inspection complements the statutory requirements but does not supersede them.

46 C.F.R. § 15.705

(a) . . . . The establishment of adequate watches is the responsibility of the vessel's master. The Coast Guard interprets the term "watch" to be the direct performance of vessel operations, whether deck or engine, where such operations would routinely be controlled and performed in a scheduled and fixed rotation. The performance of maintenance or work necessary to the vessel's safe operation on a daily basis does not in itself constitute the establishment of a watch. The minimum safe manning levels specified in a vessel's certificate of inspection takes into consideration routine maintenance requirements and ability of the crew to perform all operational evolutions, including emergencies, as well as those functions which may be assigned to persons in watches.

> (b) Subject to exceptions, 46 U.S.C. 8104 requires that when a master ... establishes watches for the licensed individuals, sailors, coal passers, firemen, oilers and watertenders, the personnel shall be "divided, when at sea, into at least three watches and shall be kept on duty successively to perform ordinary work incident to the operation and management of the vessel." The Coast Guard interprets "sailors" to mean those members of the deck department other than licensed officers, whose duties involve the mechanics of conducting the vessel on its voyage, such as helmsman (wheelsman), lookout, etc., and which are necessary to the maintenance of a continuous watch. "Sailors" is not interpreted to include able seamen and ordinary seamen not performing these duties.

Former 46 C.F.R. § 157.20-5(a)

> The requirement for division into watches applies only to those classes of the crew specifically named in [46 U.S.C. § 8104(d)].

46 C.F.R. § 15.715

> (a) Coast Guard acceptance of automated systems to replace specific personnel or to reduce overall crew requirements is predicated upon the capabilities of the system demonstrated and a planned maintenance program which ensures continued reliability and safe operation of the vessel.

> (b) The OCMI considers the capabilities of an automated system in establishing initial manning levels; however, until the system is proven reliable, a manning level adequate to operate in a continuously attended mode will be specified on a vessel's COI. It remains the responsibility of the vessel's master to determine when a continuous watch is necessary.

46 C.F.R. § 15.810

> (a) The minimum number of licensed mates required to be carried on every inspected self-propelled seagoing and Great Lakes vessel and every inspected seagoing passenger vessel is as follows:
>
> > (1) Vessels of 1000 gross tons or more—three licensed mates (except when on a voyage of less than 400 miles from port of departure to port of final destination—two licensed mates).
> >
> > (2) Vessels of 100 or more gross tons but less than 1000 gross tons—two licensed mates (except vessels of at least 100 but less than 200 gross tons on voyages which do not exceed 24 hours in duration—one licensed mate).
>
> (c) The OCMI may increase the minimum number of mates indicated in (a) of this section where it is deemed the vessel's characteristics, route, or other operating conditions create special circumstances requiring an increase.
>
> (d) The Commandant will consider reductions to the number of mates required by this section when special circumstances allowing a vessel to be safely operated can be demonstrated.

46 C.F.R. § 15.815

> (a) Each person in the required complement of licensed deck individuals on inspected vessels of 300 gross tons or over which are radar equipped, shall hold a valid endorsement as radar observer.

46 C.F.R. § 15.820

> (a) There must be an individual holding an appropriate license as chief engineer or a license authorizing service as chief engineer employed on board the following inspected mechanically propelled vessels:
>
> > (1) seagoing or Great Lakes vessels of 200 gross tons and over.

46 C.F.R. § 15.825

> An individual in charge of an engineering watch on a mechanically propelled, seagoing, documented vessel of 200 gross tons

or over, other than an individual described in 15.820 must hold an appropriate license authorizing service as an assistant engineer. The OCMI determines the minimum number of licensed engineers required for the safe operation of inspected vessels.

46 C.F.R. § 15.830

Radio officers are required on certain merchant vessels of the U.S. The determination of when a radio officer is required is based on FCC requirements.

46 C.F.R. § 15.840

(b) Able seamen are rated as: unlimited, limited, special, offshore supply vessel, sail and fishing industry. 46 U.S.C. 7312 specifies the catagories of able seamen (i.e., unlimited, limited) necessary to meet the requirements of 46 U.S.C. 8702.

(c) It is the responsibility of the master or person in charge to ensure that the able seamen in the service of the vessel meet the requirements of 46 U.S.C. 7312 and 8702.

46 C.F.R. § 15.850

The requirements for the maintenance of proper lookout are specified in Rule 5 of the International Regulations for Preventing Collisions at Sea, 1972 and Rule 5 of the Inland Navigation Rules Act of 1980 (33 U.S.C. 2005). Lookout is a function to be performed by a member of a navigational watch.

Part III: ADMINISTRATIVE PROVISIONS

A. MARINE SAFETY MANUAL

3 MSM § 21

B. *Deck Engine Mechanic, Engineman, Oiler, And Junior Engineer.* The ratings of "deck engine mechanic," "engineman," and "junior engineer" are not required on the Certificate of Inspection (COI). The minimum manning requirements are prescribed by the officer in charge marine inspection (OCMI) in accordance with 46 C.F.R. [§ 15.501]. For the engineroom, these will usually include a number of oilers. However, if the owner, operator, agent, or master of an automated or partially automated vessel requests that the vessel's complement includes a deck engine mechanic or engineman, the COI will carry the requirement for "Oilers" and a notation that "junior engineers, deck engine mechanics, or enginemen may be substituted for one or more oilers." [NOTE: Employment of these ratings as substitutions for oilers does *not* remove them from the watchstanding provisions of 46 U.S.C. 8104 and 46 C.F.R. [§ 15.705].]

C. *Maintenanceperson.* A maintenanceperson (any rating, either deck or engine) may be required on the COI for vessels having reduced crews, due to automation or installed laborsaving devices. The OCMI may determine that such personnel are necessary for the maintenance and safe operation of automation systems or to perform labor essential for the safe operation of the vessel. Maintenancepersons may be identified by departmental affiliation (deck maintenanceperson, engine maintenanceperson) or by no affiliation, in which case the master has the discretion to determine how to best utilize the person.

3 MSM § 22

A. *Authority To Set Hours of Duty.* 46 U.S.C. 8104 provides for the division of seagoing and Great Lakes merchant vessel crews into a minimum of three watches while at sea, with no more than 8 hours of work required in 1 day; for radiotelegraph operators, this requirement applies only when three or more radio officers are required. . . . [NOTE: In accordance with an opinion of the Attorney General dated 5 October 1937 (39 *Op. Att'y Gen.* 112), the word "day" in the predecessor to 46 U.S.C. 8104 was construed to mean a calendar day of 24 hours, commencing at midnight, and there is no reason to alter this interpretation.] The setting of the watches is the responsiblity of the master.

B. *Watchstanding Categories.* For purposes of applying the provisions of 46 U.S.C. 8104, unlicensed ratings shall be divided into successive watches and employed for the performance of ordinary work incident to the operation of the vessel, as follows:

1. *Deck Department.* Able Seaman (AB), Ordinary Seaman.

2. *Engine Department.* Oiler, Watertender, Fireman, Coal Passer.

3. *Radio Department.* Radio Operator (when three or more radio officers are employed).

C. *Required Work.* Seamen may not be required to work more than 8 hours in any day, except in cases of emergencies that affect the safety of the vessel, life, or property. This provision does not prohibit seamen from working overtime *voluntarily* (i.e., without direct or indirect coercion). It is not anticipated that long hours of overtime will be performed by crewmembers to the detriment of the vessel, their well-being, or environmental safety. To determine whether excessive hours are being worked, the officer in charge, marine inspection (OCMI) must decide how much of the work performed was actually required in the vessel's operation. Commandant (G-MVP) shall be advised of any changes considered necessary to a vessel's existing manning level, and shall be provided appropriate documentation to ensure that manning level modifications are applied to all vessels in a class, if necessary (see 46 U.S.C. 8104 for provisions specifically applicable to documented tugs on the Great Lakes).

D. *Time "On Duty."* A ship's officer who serves as nightmate while the ship is in port is considered to be "on duty" *whether or not* engaged in work during that time. The number of hours during which the officer is aboard in such circumstances must be figured in determining the number of hours worked during that day. Similarly, a mariner who has worked aboard ship during the day and stays aboard with the watch section at night, on call in case of fire or an emergency, is considered "on duty" within the meaning of 46 U.S.C. 8104. The statutory prohibition precluding more than 8 hours required work per day is considered to apply to those officers and crew serving in a night relief watch. The presumption is that, by accepting such employment, the night watch has *voluntarily* assumed the additional duty.

E. *Maintenance And Repair Personnel.* Maintenance personnel in the deck and engine departments generally are not included in a watch system. As there is no statutory requirement for titles of the crew's positions to be identical to those stated on the Certificate of Inspection (COI), some investigation may be needed to determine the employment of a mariner should this question arise. Generally on standard non-automated vessels, deck maintenance personnel are not required by the COI, in that such duties are only remotely concerned with the safe navigation of the vessel; any deck rating or licensed officer can serve in a deck "maintenance" position. The same can be said of engine maintenance personnel. Engine maintenance personnel may be any rating in the engine department.

3 MSM § 23

A. *Automated Vessels.*

1. *General.* Insofar as manning proposals based upon varying degrees of automation are concerned, the Commandant will review all proposals objectively. Reductions in manning scales shall be granted when they will not detract fron the safe navigation of the vessel.

B. *Navigation and Vessel Inspection Circulars*

   1. NVIC 1-69: Automated Main and Auxiliary Machinery.

   2. NVIC 7-73: Main Propulsion Boiler Automation.

   3. NVIC 6-84: Automated Main and Auxiliary Machinery, Supplemental Guidance

      NVICs may be obtained from:
      Commanding Officer
      Coast Guard Marine Safety Center
      400 7th Street, S.W.
      Washington, D.C. 20590-0001

C. *Miscellaneous Administrative Guidance*

   1. Commandant (G-MVP-4) Letter 16712 of Oct. 14, 1988 re "Information Concerning Merchant Vessel Manning." Attached.

Index

157